D0828126

So You Want to Be a Special Education Teacher...?

Hold On, You're In For A Wild Ride!
but rewarding

by Jim Yerman

Copyright © 2001. Jim Yerman.

All rights reserved under International and Pan-American Conventions. Printed in the United States of America. Except as permitted under the United States Copyright Act of 1976, no part of this publication may be reproduced or distributed in any form or by any means, or stored in a data base or retrieval system, without the prior written permission of the author.

All marketing and publishing rights guaranteed to and reserved by

FUTURE HORIZONS INC.

721 W. Abram Street
Arlington, TX 76013

800.489.0727 Toll Free
817.277.0727
817.277.2270 Fax

www.FHautism.com
email: info@FHautism.com

ISBN   1-885477-74-0

For Deborah
Love, Me

For Bryan, Ali, and Ryan
Love, Dad

For Damien and Taylor
Love, Pop-Pop

Acknowledgements

*T*hank you, Mom and Dad, the first teachers I ever had.

Thank you, Deborah. You're the person I want to see when I open my eyes each morning and before I close them each night.

Thank you, Bryan, Ali, and Ryan for teaching me the ropes of the most difficult job I've ever had, the job of father.

Thank you, Damien and Taylor, for teaching me the ropes of the easiest job I've ever had, being a grandpa.

Thank you, Maggie. In a brief time you formed the framework for my entire teaching career.

Thank you, Brenda, Dolly, Debbie, Fran, & Jan. You were always more than mere assistants. When my class ran smoothly I had you to thank. When I listened, you have been wonderful teachers.

Thank you, Phil and Lee, for your kindness, your laughter and your friendship.

Thank you to the parents of my students. I remain in awe of your commitment, determination, spirit, dedication, and your love. Thank you for entrusting your children to my care and for teaching me more than can ever be written in a book.

Thank you to my students; you were really my teachers. You have given my life perspective. Thank you for your patience with me over the years. I only hope I have enriched your lives as much as you've enriched mine.

Thank you, Wayne Gilpin, my publisher. You encouraged me to keep believing in myself; I did. Thank you for believing in me also.

Finally, thank you, Veronica Palmer, my editor. Your enthusiasm and support made this process easy and fun. Thank you for polishing my words and helping them to shine.

Contents

Preface

*W*ith friends of mine making more money than I will ever make and receiving benefits I will never see, why am I teaching? With athletes being paid unfathomable amounts of money to hit or catch or run, why did I choose teaching in the first place? With schools becoming dangerous, class sizes skyrocketing and paperwork swelling, why do I continue to teach? I won't ever be famous and I certainly won't ever be rich.

Sure, I have my dreams.

I'm sitting at a large oak table in a conference room of some reclusive billionaire.

Lawyer for the billionaire: "Tell Mr. Yerman we are willing to offer him $5 million a year with a $500,000 signing bonus, and a new house, but he'd have to start on Monday. This is a particularly difficult classroom."

My agent would look at me.

Me (whispering to the agent and trying to act nonchalant): "What about the car and Fridays?"

My agent: "Mr. Yerman is intrigued by your offer, but a school system in California has offered him this same deal with every other Friday off and use of a county car."

Spokesman for the billionaire (after conferring with his associates): "Yes. Tell Mr. Yerman we will up our offer to include every Friday off and a new car."

As I lean over to my agent he puts his hand on my shoulder, already anticipating my response and says: "His choice of colors?"

Spokesman for the billionaire: "His choice."

My agent will look at me, I'd nod and we'd have a deal.

Outside the building my agent would receive a call from Nike asking me to endorse a new shoe made just for me, the Air Teacher. After he hangs up with Nike he receives another call.

"They want you on a Wheaties box, Jim."

I smile as I descend the steps.

"Biography" will run a documentary on my life. There'd be interviews with people from my past. My successes, my failures, my comedies and my tragedies would be examined. It would be heartwarming.

I'd adorn the covers of *Newsweek, Time* and *People* magazines.

People would run up to me on the street asking for autographs.

I'd make the normal television appearances: "Today", "Leno", "Letterman", and "Oprah".

Just as I get to the part where I am giving Oprah a hug, I hear a voice that interrupts my reverie—

"Jim, Janice wet her pants again, Sandy's parents want to know why she came home with dirt on her sleeve, and the front office wants to know if you finished the paperwork on Laura yet."

Back to the reality, the everyday reality that is teaching.

The truth is, I love what I do and I work hard at teaching, but so do a lot of other people who must have similar fantasies. To me, it is all a matter of perspective.

Perspective, by definition, is ambiguous and ever changing. It is relative to where you are in your life at any particular moment.

I have often marveled at artists who have mastered the art of perspective. Being able to place every image in the correct space on the canvas, at precisely the right moment, can be beautiful. Being able to do this in life can be difficult.

Occasionally, I have fallen prey to the allure of materialism or recognition. Luckily, at those times when I have succumbed, life has presented me with an experience that yanks me back to reality.

Recently two simultaneous events highlighted this lesson for me, yet again.

I was nominated for a national award, attached to which was a good deal of money. Normally I shun such encumbrances but I decided to try for this award and its fame. I even found myself hoping I would receive it and, worse, planning what I would say and do when I won.

When my wife Deborah and I returned from a summer vacation in North Carolina, the Award Committee's letter was waiting for me. Nervously, I opened it and read how they were thankful for so many applications, but unfortunately not everyone could win. "Not everyone" meaning me. I didn't have much time to lament, though. As I opened the letter I was listening to our messages on our answering machine and discovered that Phil, a dear friend of ours, had surgery while we were away. Cancer was found in the tissue of his left leg and it had to be amputated above the knee to save his life.

I immediately went to see Phil and Lee, his wife and partner, who I knew would be at the hospital. I found them frightened, but happy that Phil was still alive. We laughed, we cried and we reminisced. During my visit, their daughter called and while I sat there bathed in this wonderful couple's sorrow and happiness, that award didn't seem important at all.

When visiting hours ended I got up to leave and walk Lee to her car. I looked back to see these two gentle, worn souls, who were about to celebrate their 60th year together, strain to kiss. Lee, who walked with a cane for support, was shaking unsteadily as she leaned over the hospital bed to kiss Phil. Phil strained to stay upright and balance where there once was a leg. I walked over to them and gently pushed their heads together, allowing their lips to meet.

I have been blessed with moments like these in my life; moments that cleanse my soul, rejuvenate my spirit and help renew my perspective.

In truth, I didn't set out to teach autistic students. I didn't aspire to it from the time I was a child nor did I receive a divine calling. It was much simpler for me. I observed a class when I was in college, found the students enchanting and before I knew it, had been teaching for over 20 years. Somewhere along the way I came to the realization that my students, these unique and fascinating individuals, had as much to teach me as I did them.

I have heard it said that there are two main differences between the high-priced athlete and a teacher. The first is that only a few athletes can compete at such a high skill level, whereas teachers are a dime a dozen. The second is that people won't pay to watch someone teach, whereas they will fill stadiums to watch star athletes. (Perhaps a third difference is that they don't allow beer in the public schools.)

My perspective is a little different. In one of these jobs you begin every new day with wild anticipation, wondering how you will react to what comes your way.

Will you be up to the challenge? Will you get a hit, or even better, a home run, or will you strike out? You are determined to do your best because you know how important you are to the team and what it means. Your life is focused and you can't think of any other place you'd rather be.

The other job is just a bunch of men playing a game.

In one of these jobs, people fill stadiums and pay to watch you play. They cheer your successes and ridicule your failures. Every action is scrutinized, but soon forgotten, as the next game or season takes place.

In the other job, only you and a handful of people are watching. You learn to revel in small successes and persevere through the failures. You will experience sadness and sorrow, and learn about acceptance. The charm of an innocent smile will warm your heart. You may become blinded by hope and angered by your incompetence. Innumerable challenging situations will make you confront your own inadequacies and bring out your strengths. Through it all you will never stop chasing the little everyday miracles in your seemingly ordinary life. Yet, what you do will never be forgotten.

As you read this book you may wonder how I can laugh and find humor amidst the anguish that is sometimes autism. Why don't I talk about how unfair it is for my students to have such a challenging condition?

I certainly don't possess all the answers. I cannot cure their autism, nor can I make life fair. But I can accept my students for who they are and help them and their families balance out the sorrow with laughter and fun. We learn, we cry, we get excited, we win, we lose and we laugh...together.

Isn't that what living should be?

Sure, money would be nice. But in this ever-changing mixed up world, when my career is over I'd rather people remember me as a good father and husband and teacher and friend, not for how much money I made. I want to be someone my children and my friends are proud of, and someone my students and their parents will have been proud to know. Then I truly will have been blessed and my life will have meant something.

After spending a lifetime with Deborah, if I still try as hard to kiss her as Lee did Phil that day in the hospital, I won't have any trouble telling people just how rich I am.

The Times They are a'Changing

I graduated from high school in 1970, which meant I was a child of the 60's. It was a time when the winds of change were whipping across our country. Long hair and hippies were changing the way we looked at fashion, Woodstock changed how we looked at music and drugs, Vietnam changed how we looked at war and peace. The feminist movement changed how we viewed women, and Kent State and Watergate forever changed how we viewed ourselves.

At that time the world of autism was made up of frightened parents, a few paragraphs of text in psychology textbooks, and individuals more often seen as psychotic than autistic. Students with disabilities were nowhere to be found in public schools. Why? Perhaps as a society we weren't ready to acknowledge them yet. Perhaps because they were all locked away in concrete institutions or kept behind closed doors at home, deprived of all social contact.

Even as late as 1976, Dr. Bruno Bettelheim expounded his theory that autism was caused by bad mothering. Of course, he was wrong and his theory has since been proven false. But it was as if he had poured ink onto the fabric of autism. It stained everything it touched and did not rub out for a very long time.

As the winds of change were blowing through our world, they slowly crept into the educational sector, too. We started seeing an attitudinal shift toward educating students with disabilities, including autism. I was hired to teach such a class and it is within this emergent climate that this book begins.

It was a time when concepts such as person-first language, mainstreaming, full inclusion and person-centered planning existed only in the minds of individuals not yet born. Our hallways echoed the spoken and unspoken sentiments of that time: "retard", "second class citizens", "handicapped", "moron" and "idiot." The prognosis for a child with autism was grim. There was nothing positive about the disability and it was unfathomable that any child could grow to contribute in any way. In the schools and in the community, people gawked, they pointed, they snickered and sneered. Fear of the unknown colored the glasses they wore, and nothing was more unknown than how to teach students with autism.

Luckily, paralleling the evolution of our social consciousness was growth and change in techniques and educational practices. I was educated as a behaviorist and believed I could "train" my students using reinforcement and aversive techniques much the same way we trained animals. I was wrong. Throwing much of my "book learning" out of the window, I realized these were complex people trying their best to exist in a complex world. I learned that a balance between compassion and discipline, understanding and instruction was much more beneficial than any class I had ever taken in college.

As a teacher, I have lived with autism for the past 26 years. I like to think I have accepted my students for the unique persons they are. For me, autism is just part of their being; it is not who they are. In many ways, my students have become part of my family. And, as with a family, I have learned to laugh and find humor in the absurdity of our everyday situations, for they certainly exist!

This book chronicles some of those situations. Most of them are humorous, some are sad and a few are downright surreal. But they're all real and for me this has been a refreshing and honest way of talking about autism. Each student, each story has taught me an important lesson that in the end became the real reason for telling them to you.

If you embrace teaching students with autism you become free to cry, to get angry, or to laugh out loud. In a society where we are afraid to say anything for fear of upsetting one group or another, I am not ashamed to get angry or cry or laugh at the predicaments that have arisen in my life. My intention is not to make fun of my students. To the contrary, it is to show the normal humor in our everyday lives. I believe it is a compliment to how far we have come in embracing the autism community that we can laugh at their foibles just as we laugh at our own.

I was lucky to be on the crest of this wave of acceptance and change through the early and middle years of my career. This book rides with me from Ohio to Florida, from working in an integrated university school, into a center for only handicapped students and back to a regular middle and high school.

It's a wave I am still riding and I can't wait to see where we end up.

[scan in and place his signature]

Jim Yerman
May 2001

Chapter One
So You Want to be a
Special Education Teacher?

"So you want to be a teacher?" I heard a woman ask as I walked onto the playground of the Kent University School.

"That's what I'm hoping to find out," I replied, trying to locate the speaker. Before I was successful she spoke again.

"Well, over there's a good place to start."

My eyes fell onto a petite young woman with brown curly hair and round chestnut eyes. She was pointing. I followed the line of her arm and noticed a little boy running along the outside of the fenced playground toward the street.

"His name is Tommy," the woman said. "He's a runner. You need to get him and bring him back."

Unsure if this was real or some cruel joke, I hesitated.

"And you'd better hurry, he's getting away."

I looked at Tommy who, by now, had reached the street.

"I'll get him," I assured the woman and took off.

"Good luck, he's pretty fast!" The voice faded as I sped away.

Tommy was 50 yards ahead and showed no signs of slowing down. I wasn't worried. I was young and strong. I diligently narrowed the gap until he was within reach.

"This wasn't too hard," I said to myself with a modicum of pride. I extended my arms and readied to make the capture.

As I closed in, Tommy looked over his shoulder, smiled, then turned and spurted away in another gear. I realized he was toying with me and enjoying this little predicament he had created.

It's curious what enters a person's mind at a time like this, but suddenly I began to think about running.

I enjoy running. I awake before everyone else in my family and run two miles every day. There is a freedom, a catharsis I feel when running. I can run as fast or as slowly as I choose. My mind is free to think, or to not think and simply enjoy the experience.

As I was running in this unconventional two-man race my mind drifted back to second grade, at St. Barnabas Catholic school. I was in love with a classmate named Samantha (at least as much as a seven-year-old could love). My friends, however, didn't share my level of maturity on the subject. They told me if I wanted to stay friends with them I needed to sneak up behind Samantha and give her a push. At seven years old I was not accustomed to making such difficult decisions. I chose to give Samantha the old heave ho.

It probably would have turned out better if not for my poor timing. I chose a day when Samantha wore a pretty, puffy white dress trimmed with lace—not the usual Catholic school uniform. With the gang watching my every move and offering a tacit amount of courage, I crept up behind Samantha, shoved her, then turned and ran away as fast as I could. I was running with a joy much like Tommy's when I looked back at my friends. They were not waiting and watching me anymore. They too were running, but not with unbridled pleasure. Instead, they were running fast, screaming and waving their hands over their heads.

Louie Lipchick, my best friend, turned around.

"Jim," he yelled. "Look." He pointed back toward the scene of the crime.

I stopped and turned around.

It seems the little shove I thought I had given Samantha was really a severe push. It propelled her headfirst into an extremely muddy puddle in the middle of the playground. I never heard the splash.

Before I had time to realize what I'd done—let alone apologize for it—I was brought directly to the office of the head priest, Father McGonahey. We all believed that Father McGonahey was a direct descendant of God himself. No one was more pious, blessed, or divine than Father McGonahey and no one brought more fear into the hearts and minds of the pupils of St. Barnabas.

"What do you have to say for yourself, young man?" Father McGonahey boomed.

I was too busy cowering to look directly into his holiness' eyes. Moreover, I wasn't sure what would happen if I did. I wasn't about to take the chance.

"I don't know, Sir. I'm sorry." I whispered incredulously.

"Well, such an indiscretion cannot go unpunished, as you know. What do you think I should do, Mr. Yerman?"

Sure, I was only in the second grade. But even at such a tender age I knew how to beg. I knelt down at the Father's feet and said, "I don't know, Sir. I throw myself on your holiness' mercy."

In retrospect, perhaps "your holiness" was a bit much, as my punishment came swiftly and severely. I was brought into the office at St. Barnabas where, during afternoon announcements, my sordid deed was broadcast for the entire school to hear. Then, with the P.A. still on, I was spanked by Father McGonahey until I apologized. The good Father must have been a little hard of hearing. I apologized immediately, yet he kept spanking me anyway. Perhaps he couldn't hear me over the sound of his hand repeatedly hitting my rear. He kept swatting away until he was finally satisfied with my repentance.

"Now, let this be a lesson to the rest of you," Father McGonahey said as my punishment ended; and so it was.

To add insult to injury, I had to recite so many Hail Marys and Our Fathers—standard Catholic penance—that I held the St. Barnabas record for two years. That record was finally broken by Chris Johnson after he was caught writing "Father McGonahey is a St. BarnabASS" in soap on the windows of the rectory one Halloween.

If my penance wasn't chastisement enough, Samantha never spoke to me again and our relationship never found its way out of that mud puddle.

My mind drifted to another time, when I was running away from the school I attended. I had transferred from St. Barnabas to public school in the fifth grade. There was an ignoble tradition in Twinsburg: every year a group of seniors would paint the side of the school. At that time (a long time ago), graffiti was pretty tame. Sayings like "Go

Seniors" and "Tigers Rule" were standard. While no one was quite sure when this tradition began, in that year the custom fell to my group of friends to continue it. Who were we to buck tradition?

One night after dark we met at my house, packed our supplies, trekked through the woods and painted our hearts out. As we ran back through the woods that evening, with no one the wiser, there was joy and laughter in our run. We were spurred on by the feeling of success and having escaped capture. In some way I knew what Tommy must have been feeling as he remained just out of my reach.

In spite of our precision and planning, we made three mistakes that night. First, I outfitted my troops with enamel based paint instead of the easy-to-clean acrylic. (Who knew?) Second, I hadn't realized this was the day before the county track meet and our school was the host. (I repeat, who knew?) And third, I told Rose Bushnell. Rose was a friend with a very innocent and truthful heart. The next morning, when the principal appealed for someone to come forward and reveal the perpetrators of this heinous crime, Rose snapped like a wishbone at Thanksgiving. Once again, I found myself on the wrong side of school administration. My friends and I were rounded up and, as part of our punishment, made to pay for the cleaning. We learned valuable lessons in friendship, right and wrong, economics and sand blasting.

"Let this be a lesson to the rest of you," Principal Riddick said over the P.A. system. And it was. Once again, it was!

Moving as quickly as my feet, my mind raced on to Muskingum College, a small liberal arts institution nestled in the foothills of southern Ohio. I was running across the campus one day, trying to decide upon my major. I was enjoying a cleansing run when I ran into Professor Titus.

"And just where are you going with yourself, Mr. Yerman?" Professor Titus asked.

This was way too synchronistic for me.

"I'm going to major in Psychology, Dr. Titus, that's what," I declared proudly.

"That's nice, Mr. Yerman. But I meant, are you heading to the cafeteria or the library?"

It was too late. My mind was made up. However, there was one little problem with the decision. How many people do you know who make a living with a B.A. in psychology? My point exactly. So my only recourse, after graduation, was to head back to school. I enrolled in graduate school at Kent State University and once again began the task of finding a major. Education seemed a likely candidate. I was intrigued that Kent State University School had a class for autistic students.

"Why don't you run on over and see how you like it," my professor said to me.

Now here I was, in the fall of 1977, in hot pursuit of a young autistic student who, I was convinced, was an Olympic marathon runner.

Tommy was enjoying the run. He ran with reckless abandon, continually laughing, arms flailing, feet kicking up dust, and head bobbing with delight. In contrast, I was sweating, my legs hurt, and I was breathing so hard I sounded like a foghorn. But it had become a matter of ego. Straining with every ounce of strength I had left I closed in, seized Tommy and carried him to the grass on the side of the road.

I smiled at my captive, wanting him to know he had nothing to fear. I had a way with children and was confident my reassuring smile would accomplish its goal. Tommy took one look at my smile, bit my hand and was off again in an instant. This kid could go from zero to 60 in no time at all! Undaunted and more determined than ever, I joined the chase, caught him and dragged him back to the playground. Once there, Tommy ran to the swing and began the solitary play so characteristic of many autistic students.

"Nice capture," his teacher said. "I usually don't catch him until he's turned the corner onto Central. By the way, my name is Maggie."

"Jim. Nice to meet you."

I spent that year volunteering in Maggie's classroom and discovered that teaching these unique individuals was, indeed, what I wanted to do.

As fate would have it, after graduating from Kent the following summer, I was chosen to teach a new autistic class in the Kent University School. My classroom would be next door to Maggie's.

Over 25 years have passed since my inauspicious debut on the streets of Kent, Ohio. I have spent them not only as a teacher of autistic students, but as their student as well. Teaching is a noble profession. If we are lucky, we keep our students happy and they grow into more independent citizens. When we are truly fortunate, we learn new things about ourselves along the way.

The stories in this book illustrate what wonderful teachers autistic students have been for me in my life. The very first lesson I learned that day in Kent has remained with me ever since. I learned I had better hold on tight, because I was in for one wild ride!

Chapter Two
Ready or Not, Here We Come!

*T*he University School was operated cooperatively by the Kent City Schools and Kent State University as a training facility for teachers. It was an unconventional place to begin teaching. Attached to my classroom was an observation room where people could watch and learn from what I was doing. Only three months earlier I had been using Maggie's observation room to watch her. Now I was the one being scrutinized.

Without a doubt, this set-up contributed to my anxiety that sooner or later, someone was going to guess that I didn't know what I was doing. I even had a recurring dream that, like a former 60's terrorist who lived in fear that someday his real identity would be revealed, the authorities would enter my classroom and take me away.

"Mr. Yerman, you need to come with us."

I'd look at their faces, immediately recognize them, bow my head and go quietly, a wave of relief flowing through my body.

But maybe, just maybe, it was Bobby who fueled my assumption that I really didn't know what I was doing.

In the beginning, the observation room did not intimi-date me. At that time, information on teaching students with autism was scarce. I was armed with the latest philosophy, materials and techniques in the field. I knew as much as any-one. I was young, eager, energetic and full of the precarious confidence that comes with innocence and inexperience.

Like most new teachers, I set up my first classroom as a captivating place. My bulletin boards were covered with cartoons, smiling faces, and a myriad of colors. My six students' desks were cleaned and placed in three pre-cise rows of two. My desk, adorned with a philodendron, was centrally located in front of the room.

Everything was perfect. I awaited my first students with a mix of apprehension and anticipation. They would feel great in this classroom. The learning that would emanate from it was going to be downright scary. I even hung welcome signs in the observation room, so they could watch the glorious events unfold.

I stood in my doorway, brimming with expectation, as Bobby and his mother approached. As they walked down the hallway toward my room, I smiled and waved. I had been waiting for this moment for a long time.

Bobby, who was 16 years old, stood 5'10" tall and weighed over 200 pounds. He had blond hair and blue eyes and took no notice of me as he scurried into the room.

I introduced myself to his mother.

"Hi, I'm Mr. Yerman," I said. "You must be Bobby's mother, Mrs. Green."

"Oh, I am sorry," she said, ignoring my greeting. "I for-got to give Bobby his medicine this morning. You should be careful. He might have an accident."

"An accident?" I was confused, "what kind of—"

Before I could finish and within the time it took to say these words, Bobby had stripped everything from my bulletin boards, slid my philodendron onto the floor and somehow managed to push all my desks into a jumble in the center of the room.

Slowly, I walked in and surveyed the scene. It was similar to one in *Gone with the Wind,* when the camera pans back and we see the horrors of the war. All my desks were strewn about, seemingly crying for help; all my materials, my philodendron, and my hopes scattered across the floor.

"Oh, I forgot to tell you," Bobby's mom said. "Bobby doesn't like anything on the walls."

She shrugged. A crooked grin formed on her face.

Meanwhile, Bobby had found a comfortable spot on the floor and was playing with a blob of clay.

I walked over to give him my first lesson in behavior management. I had to show him that his behavior was unacceptable. I wasn't going to let him, no matter how big he was, come into my room, tear it apart, and get rewarded by being allowed to play. I'd show him. After all, I had the degree in psychology. I had the superior intelligence. From where I stood, I held all the cards and I was about to seize control.

"Bobby," I demanded, "you give me that clay right now and go sit at your desk."

Bobby handed me the clay, ran to a corner and began screaming.

"Well, at least I got the clay," I thought to myself, contentedly.

At that precise moment I realized that I didn't have any clay in my classroom. Bobby had handed me a clump of his own excrement.

"I told you he might have an accident," his mother said. "By the way, I'm late for work. Call me if you need anything."

And she was off.

I was left with my room in a shambles, my first student howling and cowering in the corner, and my hands full of crap.

I stood there for a minute, mentally searching through my college education for an answer. Nothing in school had prepared me for this situation.

"Oh well," I said to myself. "At least it can't get any worse."

Over the years in this profession, I have learned never to utter these words, as it invariably does. Today was no exception.

As if on cue, Mark Mulvaney popped his head in the door.

"Jim," he said smiling, "I have some people here who would like to meet you."

Mark was the school psychologist and the person responsible for setting up the autistic program in the Kent City Schools. He was also my boss and thought it would be a good public relations move to bring in some visitors on my first day. Joining him were the superintendent of the Kent City schools, the mayor of Kent, and one councilwoman.

"Jim is our newest teacher," Mark bragged, seemingly oblivious to the chaos reigning around him. "He joins Maggie. We are looking for great things from this program in the future."

"Future being the operative word," I said to myself.

Mark hesitated, as an awareness of what was happening finally took hold.

I smiled a half-hearted smile and looked for some-place to dispose of my ill-gotten booty.

"Er—excuse me, Mark, but my hands are a little full right now."

Quickly I rushed to the bathroom within my room, disposed of the droppings and washed my hands.

"Hello," I said enthusiastically, as I finished drying my hands and turned to my illustrious guests. "It's a plea-sure to meet you."

But only Bobby was left in the room and he was still screaming. Mark and my guests were gone. I imagined so, too, was their regard for my teaching ability.

I didn't have time to worry about what they thought, however, as more members of my class began arriving.

Raymond, a tall, meek young man with brown hair and dark rimmed glasses was first. Paul, a young man of average height, with ebony hair that contrasted with his ivory skin, followed him. Next came Chester, a short boy with curly blond hair, Coke-bottle thick glasses, and a wonderful smile.

I barely had enough time to rearrange the room and seat these students when my last two pupils entered the room.

Linda was a tiny girl, no more than three feet tall, who couldn't have weighed more than 50 pounds. She had a red, unkempt mop-top hairdo and wore horn-rimmed glasses that sat askew on her tiny head. She quickly ran to my desk and parked herself underneath it.

Following her was Marty. He arrived in a helmet and a straight jacket, because otherwise he was constantly and relentlessly attempting to hit himself in the head or bang his head against walls and desks. His mother guided him into a desk. He sat down and proceeded to bang his head against it.

The last person to arrive was my assistant, Brenda, who had been waiting for my students' bus to arrive. Brenda was in her late 20's, with long black hair and a beautifully sculptured face.

We stood there for a moment looking at each other. Next we scanned the scene of what was to be our first class. Before us were six students, three of them in their seats and sitting quietly, one in his seat but agonizingly thumping his head on the top of his desk, one in the corner screaming and another under my desk.

I smiled at Brenda, hoping she would not sense my reluctance or see the dismay on my face.

"Are you ready for this?" I asked.

"I guess so," she replied.

Together we leaped into teaching like two uncertain children jumping into a lake when they are learning how to swim.

There is a special feeling that surrounds the first time we do something. Memories of our "firsts" remain with us forever. Our first bike, first kiss, first job, first house, are turning points in our lives. They make up who we are and who we become. Looking back, that first day was a great day because we survived it. It taught me that there are no easy answers when dealing with students with autism. They are too complex and too individual to follow any set pattern or theory. What works for nine students may not work for the tenth; what works for one may not work for another.

It also didn't take me long to understand that no one else had the answers, either. Everyone is searching for solutions. The best we can do is to keep trying and searching together.

I no longer wait for the authorities to enter my room and take me away. Time, experience and a modicum of success have removed such anxieties. I do, however, relive that feeling of anticipation and apprehension at the beginning of each school year. I wait at my doorstep, hoping I am prepared, hoping I will do a good job, hoping I can help my students. And ready, always ready, as Kobi Yamada states, to "take the leap and build my wings on the way down."

Chapter Three

Forget What You Learned in College

*I*n some way still unknown to researchers, the developing brain of a person with autism becomes injured. The damage affects their ability to function in and understand the world around them in a variety of ways. People with autism can exhibit a wide range of characteristics, in varying degrees of severity from mild to severe. Although there are similarities from person to person, no two cases are identical. Often treatments that work well with one individual may have no effect on another.

Imagine being trapped in a world where you can't explain an ache, a pain, a want or a need. Imagine hearing the words your parents and the people around you speak, but having no idea what they're saying. Imagine how a person who has no language or speech thinks. Do they think in pictures? Imagine just how frustrating and angry you might be, given these challenges.

There are many people with autism who do not speak and whose understanding of language is seriously limited. It's as if they're forever doomed to walk as visitors in a foreign country, where they will never fully understand what is going on. At this level of impairment we often see aggression, or self-abuse, or, and this is where the term "autism" originates, a withdrawal into themselves, three understandable reactions to their constant level of frustration.

"David, did you have a nice night?" I ask.

"Yes," comes the curt reply.

"Did you go to Burger King?"

"Yes."

"Did you eat a hamburger?"

"Yes."

"Did you eat a telephone pole?"

"Yes."

"Did you travel to Mars?"

"Yes."

Now, suppose you understand some of the things you hear, but not all. From repetition and routine you have associated some language with certain objects, acts and people. When a person talks to you, you pick up a few words but not all, and you react to the words you understand. Your restricted comprehension limits your responses to simple answers and infrequent spontaneity. You struggle to speak in the simple words you understand, and live in a constant state of bewilderment. How would you cope? You might search for answers outside the spoken words, and develop rote responses based on the tone of a person's voice. When pushed into a conversation, you might answer erroneously, unable to grasp the meaning of what is being said.

There are some people with autism whose life is in this constant state of puzzlement. They are able to understand certain words and phrases, but are confused by most language and unable to hold a complex conversation. They are destined to live in a simple, innocent world.

"What do you do?" It is a question I am asked frequently.

"I'm a teacher," I reply. "I teach autistic students."

There is the usual pause.

"It must be rewarding teaching them to draw."

In the beginning I would explain the difference between "autistic" and "artistic." I would go to great extremes to verbally paint a picture of the students I teach. After all, wasn't it my duty? However, in polite conversation I probably went too far, and people would quickly look for another conversational partner.

I have learned to read the subtleties of the situation and answer accordingly. If I sense someone is interested, really interested, not just making small talk, I discuss the details. If not, the conversation goes something like this.

"What do you do?"

"I'm a teacher; I teach autistic students."

"It must be rewarding teaching them to draw."

"Yes, it is." I say, and we both go about our business.

There are some people with autism (and at this level it is now commonly referred to as Asperger's Syndrome) who do understand language. They do not, however, understand socialization. They don't know how to interact with people and often live in inner isolation. What if you were unable to decipher, with any degree of certainty, the intricate nuances of a social situation? You might interrupt or say things that are inappropriate. You may only want to talk about one subject—incessantly, at that—and ignore people unless they are talking about it. What if you didn't understand that other people had thoughts different from your own? Given this inability to share feelings, how would you make friends?

There are other people with autism, often referred to as savants, who have highly developed and unique abilities in one specific area. I've taught a student who could draw a detailed map of the USA and label the states, rivers and counties. Another student could tell you when every horror movie ever made was released, who directed and starred in them. I've had a student who could draw and label every vegetable known to man, and one who could, given a date, tell you the corresponding day of the week. One student in our program could name the participants of every Super Bowl, who won, the score, the most valuable player and even act out the winning plays. Another knew the number and the driver of every bus he or my class ever rode and the year it came into production.

All of these students, despite their wonderful abilities, were unable to socialize appropriately and many were unable to complete simple tasks that involved thinking and reasoning. Although they were able to find happiness in their world, they had few friends, if any. Imagine your life like this. Would you be happy?

Although admittedly simplistic and general, these are the forms of autism I have come to understand over the years.

But understanding is just the beginning. I have spent my entire adult life trying to find answers that will help my students move away from their solitude and into the world, for better or for worse. The answers are as diverse as the students, and often undergo transformation.

In college, I was taught that people with autism would forever be unresponsive and could not form relationships. When I was younger, I listened to these teachings and committed them to memory, no questions asked. Now that I'm older, I've learned to hate generalities. They don't contribute to the understanding of any group of people, autistic or otherwise.

What we must do is view teachings with skepticism, ignore the generalities, and look beyond the autism. When we do, we see people just like us. I have seen some of the most engaging smiles cross my students' "unresponsive" faces. When I discovered a way to tap into the things they liked, they were fun to be around. They have good days and bad days, likes and dislikes. Each one of them is unique. Each one is trying to cope in this world given their capabilities, just like the rest of us.

I have learned it is important to make my students feel comfortable and happy first. Learning will follow.

When I began teaching I had different expectations, however. My training was in behavioral psychology and behavior modification. I had learned the behaviorist theories of B.F. Skinner and trained rats to perform in a Skinner box. In a nutshell, behaviorism teaches that behaviors are learned responses and can be taught. Initial learning takes place through continuous reinforcement and extinction through continuous aversion or punishment. Long-term learning is enhanced through intermittent reinforcement.

Behaviorist theory states that behaviors are extinguished in much the same manner. You begin by extinguishing an inappropriate behavior, then teaching an alternate appropriate behavior. At first this is done through continuous reinforcement. Once learned, it is sustained through intermittent reinforcement. Armed with this knowledge and fresh out of school, I was ready to use it in my classroom. I would extinguish the bad behaviors and substitute more appropriate ones by using behavior modification. My classroom would become a giant Skinner box.

One day Russell taught me to see things in a different light.

I was taught, and for the most part believe that teachers should expect two basic behaviors from all of our students: they must sit in their seats and they must sit quietly. Consequently, these became my two steadfast rules.

Russell was a musician. To be more exact, he was a conductor. He was of average build and stood approximately six feet tall. He had light brown wavy hair parted on the side and wore tortoise shell glasses. He was 15 years old, but looked and acted older—somewhere in the neighborhood of 65.

Russell spurned the popular rock and roll music of the day, preferring classical music and a group known as the Sons of the Pioneers. The Sons of the Pioneers, for anyone less attuned to the musical world, was the backup band for Roy Rogers. Russell's reading ability was poor and his comprehension even worse, but he knew his Sons of the Pioneers. As I've always encouraged music playing during the class day, he frequently brought in his album, with the complete story of the Sons of the Pioneers on the back.

One day I began reading their story aloud off the album jacket. Something caught my attention and I paused in mid sentence. I noticed Russell was mumbling.

I moved closer to hear him finish a sentence about the Sons of the Pioneers. As I glanced back at the album jacket, I noticed he had finished the sentence I had prematurely ended. I began to read the next sentence, paused again, and listened as Russell completed it for me. We played our little game of cat and mouse until I realized Russell had the entire cover memorized, backwards and forwards. Not only did he know the Sons, but he performed this feat with many of his classical albums as well. He was amazing.

However, Russell's memorization skill was not his most impressive musical ability. He loved his music so much—especially classical music—that at unplanned times during the day, it would overpower him. He would close his eyes and his head would begin to sway. Then his body would begin to undulate back and forth. Finally, the crescendo would be too much for him and he'd explode from his seat to begin conducting. After the finale, he'd return to his seat, open his eyes and resume the business of learning.

As innocent as this behavior was, it violated one of my major rules, sitting in his seat. Initially, by instinct, I told Russell to sit down.

"Russell, the rule is sit in your seat," I'd say.

Russell would oblige, but this saddened him. Then the music would engulf him again and up he'd go.

I am happy to report that I finally acquiesced and Russell was allowed to conduct his little heart out. He showed me that I was dealing with people, not rats, and there are no hard and fast rules with people.

Through Russell, and followed by every other student I have ever taught, I have learned about innocence. People with autism act without pretense. What you see is what you get, good or bad. I believe we are all born with this same innocence. Unfortunately, as we grow, we become more inhibited and tend to lose this wonderful quality. Society and its expectations mold us; as we become harder, our simplicity fades. Because of their autism, my students have been able to retain their innocence. It is perhaps one of their most redeeming qualities. I have Russell, his classical music and his Sons of the Pioneers to thank for teaching me to look at each person I teach as an individual, to be flexible enough to know when I am wrong, and to make a change. Russell gave me an opportunity to learn that there are things I can conduct, things I can't conduct and, more importantly, things I shouldn't conduct.

Experience teaches us by our successes to continue, and by our failures to try another way. This is a lesson I try to pass along to my students. I am a firm believer in giving my students the opportunity to succeed on their own. Inherent in this philosophy, however, is the opposite. It also gives them the opportunity to fail and make mistakes. We learn only through trial and error, and we fail only when we quit.

Speaking of trying, try as we might to find a solution to Tommy's running, I continued chasing him daily from September to October, while I volunteered in Maggie's class. We couldn't find a way to stop this urge. On the up side, however, I lost 10 pounds.

Sometimes life brings us answers in a most mysterious way.

That Halloween we were having a party and I brought in a huge mask. It was a full-length mask of a witch doctor's head and it was hideous. It was as big as I was and could be a little intimidating for anyone, let alone our students. When I came in the door with that mask on, Tommy let out a shriek that could be heard in downtown Kent. He screamed, hid under his desk, and covered his face. I quickly removed the mask and tried to relieve his anxiety by showing him it was me. Unfortunately, and to my dismay, my real face was little consolation. We removed the mask from the room and things returned to normal.

That day at recess, Tommy and I did our usual run for the roses and, as I was dragging him back into the playground, it hit me. I ran my idea by Maggie and she agreed.

The next day Tommy began his running routine, but when he reached the gate the witch doctor was there. He was startled as I jumped in front of him, blocking his way. But he was downright scared when I began jumping up and down repeating, "Ooga-booga, ooga-booga."

That's all it took. He ran back into the playground, never to run away again.

At the time, we agonized over this procedure but felt the benefits outweighed its aversive nature. As Tommy ran down the streets of Kent there was a real possibility he could get hurt. If, however, he thought the witch doctor was waiting for him, he would be afraid, but safe and sound within the protection of the playground.

The witch doctor never had to make another house call. In a way, it was a shame. It was one great mask and I did a mean Ooga Booga.

Bobby was a different story. His mom had advised me that it was a good idea to keep things off the wall and make the room as distraction free (call it drab and boring) as possible. I have never subscribed to this theory, thinking instead that the world is not a drab and colorless place. Dealing with it is something we all have to do. Therefore, it became my job to help Bobby learn to tolerate things on the wall and plants on my desk. We began by compromising. I put up a poster and Bobby didn't tear it down. By the end of the year, my room was the way I had assembled it before Hurricane Bobby hit.

Many years later—I was now teaching in Florida—one of the college students observing my class raised his hand and asked me how I had learned to use "operant conditioning" so well. I had been so far removed from academia by then that I had to confess I wasn't sure what that term meant.

We all found them funny at the time, but as I reflect back on those moments now, I thank Russell and Bobby for helping me forget some of the book smarts I learned in school. They taught me that I could learn so much more from my students than I could ever learn from a book.

Chapter Four
Be Prepared for Surprises!

*M*y first glimpse of Linda was her behind. It was a week before the first day of school and her mom wanted to bring her in to meet me and see the school.

As her mom dragged her down the hallway toward my room, I only saw her rear end as it swayed back and forth like a pendulum, occasionally bouncing off the tile. The thought crossed my mind that this was an unorthodox way to be introduced. Linda didn't talk, but it was easy to understand by her body language that she wasn't too excited to be there. I didn't know it then, but seeing Linda's behind would become one of my most cherished memories.

What Linda lacked in speech she more than made up for in spunk. And, she had an infectious smile. She would put her hand up to her glasses, hold onto one side, then a beautiful, innocent, smile would engulf her little face. It was hard to be angry at her when she smiled. The irony was that she usually flashed this smile after she had done something aggravating, or just as she was preparing to do so.

"Well, this can't be too difficult," I remember saying to myself as Mom pulled her down the hall toward my classroom. (Another of those erroneous statements I learned never to utter again.) "I'm bigger and smarter than she is."

At least I was half-right.

Using time-out rooms was an accepted behavior management practice back in those days. These were freestanding closet-like rooms built by the school district, to a standard set of specifications. They were very tall and thin with no top. The door, which locked, had large circular holes drilled into it so the student could see out. It resembled a cumbersome, drab, green armoire standing in the corner of my room.

The concept was simple. A student who exhibited an inappropriate behavior would be told the rule, put inside the time-out room for a specific amount of time, usually two to five minutes, then brought back to the activity. The hope was that the student, seeing what he or she was missing, would change the behavior. It's similar to the time-out chair we all used in raising our own children, only more institutional. Use of the time-out room was documented to ensure that the inappropriate behavior was, indeed, decreasing. Used incorrectly, however—and this is the reason for their eventual abolishment—they could become an instrument for abuse.

At that time they were the latest trend, were touted as an autistic panacea and we used them enthusiastically.

Linda did not like to sit, preferring to get up and run around every few seconds. So we decided to use the time-out procedure to extinguish this behavior. Each time she got out of her seat inappropriately, Brenda or I would catch her, tell her the rule, "sit in your seat", and put her in the time-out room for five minutes. During this time, everyone who was sitting could play a game, or have a snack. When her five minutes were up, she was brought back to her seat and we would reward her for staying there.

The moment arrived. I caught Linda and put her in time-out, but to our astonishment, she seemed to enjoy the experience. Apparently she thought she was in the changing room at the local department store. Before I could say "Gypsy Rose Lee," an article of her clothing would fly out the opening at the top of the time-out room, float gently down, and softly land somewhere in my room. Then another piece would come drifting down, and another, and another, until her panties, her final curtain, would come down. When her time had elapsed, we opened the door and there stood Linda stark naked, with one hand holding her glasses and smiling that insidious smile. Brenda would get her dressed again and we were ready to resume.

For the most part we could ignore this unusual downpour of clothing, but Linda had acute aim when it came to her panties. They always landed on Russell's head. The first three times Linda was in time-out, the result was the same. Needless to say, this was a bit disconcerting, especially to Russell.

Despite its less than successful beginning, I was determined to try the procedure a little while longer to see if it would eventually produce the desired change in behavior.

On one unusually quiet day I stopped, as I am wont to do, to enjoy what was going on in the room. Everyone was working, the students were contented, Rossini was playing on the record player, and all seemed right with the world.

Suddenly, Linda jumped from her seat and began running around the room.

"The rule is sit in your seat," I said, as I captured her and put her in time-out.

As I documented the time she had entered the room, out of the top flew her shoe. What made this odd was that it seemed to be right on beat with the cymbal crash of *The William Tell Overture,* playing in the background. Before I had time to ponder the synchronicity of the moment, up jumped Russell to conduct. Then things got downright surreal. Russell began conducting his heart out and Linda, who must have been feeling the music as well, would oblige each and every sound of the cymbals with another piece of clothing. The performance was breathtaking. It was like watching a Fourth of July show complete with coordinated music and fireworks (with Russell providing the music and Linda providing the fireworks).

Every time there was a BOOM, there was an accompanying rocket of apparel shot out the top of the time-out room. BOOM, her shorts flew out with a crescendo. BOOM, her socks were not far behind. BOOM, her blouse flew as the tempo increased. From the sublime we quickly moved to the ridiculous as—and to this day I still find this amazing—the last cymbal crashed as Linda's panties, her personal finale, shot over the top of the box and came to rest on Russell's head. He took his usual bow, removed the panties and sat back down.

We gathered Linda's clothes and Brenda took them to the time-out room to get her dressed.

"Here you go, Linda," she said, as she opened the door a crack to return the clothes.

But, Linda was not finished with her personal con-
certo yet. Apparently still energized by the music, she
bolted from the time-out room and began running
around the classroom. Brenda and I immediately gave
chase, but there were many obstacles in our path. The
least of which was the other students, whose eyes were
now popping out of their sockets. Linda bobbed and
weaved as Brenda and I lunged and missed. I was yelling
at her to stop, Brenda was yelling at her to stop, and Linda
was smiling. All the time she was smiling, as she eluded
us like a halfback running for the goal.

Finally we were able to herd her into a corner, Brenda
to her left and me on her right. Slowly we moved in for
the capture. Linda looked at Brenda, looked at me, looked
to the front of the room, then smiled. I was beginning to
hate that smile.

Linda, this tiny, naked, autistic girl had quickly
hatched a plan that would outsmart two reasonably intelligent adults (and at this point I was beginning to doubt
just how intelligent we were). She slid under the desk we
were using as an obstruction and bolted for the door to
our room, the door to the hallway and freedom.

"Linda, NO-O-O!" I implored, as I realized what she
was doing. It was too late.

She opened the door and was now running down the
hallway of the University School in her birthday suit, with
her hands raised in triumph.

"What are we going to do?" Brenda asked.

"Head her off at the pass," I said.

I yelled at Maggie to watch the rest of my students,
who were still sitting there with their mouths agape, and
we took off. As we entered the hallway we could see

Linda's bare rear end as it reached the end of the hallway and turned the corner to the stairwell. We couldn't see her smile, but I'm sure it was there.

"Follow the bouncing butt," I said.

Brenda chased after Linda as I ran to the other stairway at the end of the hall, in hopes of heading her off. It worked. She stopped when she saw me. Brenda was able to seize her, bring her back to our room and get her dressed.

I'm not quite sure when I made the decision to curtail the time-out procedure with Linda. Perhaps it was during the fireworks, or perhaps it was after lunging for her and missing. Most likely, it was while watching her moon the entire school. When didn't matter, the decision was made. I saw no need for any more documentation on the subject.

"Well, at least she didn't make it outside," I said to Brenda, as we reentered the classroom, trying to put a positive spin on the fiasco.

But my dilemma was hardly over. The rest of my class, all boys, was sitting exactly as we had left them, thunderstruck.

Paul was the first to speak.

"Hey, Mr. Yerman. Did you know you left the room open?" he said, pointing to the time-out room.

"Why no, Paul," I said. Apparently he wasn't going to mention that little thing with the naked girl.

Confidently I walked over and closed the time-out room door.

"Now, where were we?" I asked, convinced the worst was over.

"Did you notice," Paul continued.

"Notice what, Paul?" I asked, listening intently and hoping to get back to some semblance of normalcy.

"That Linda has no peter."

I was ready for math. I was ready for reading. Again I searched my college training and realized I was not prepared for this question. (At times like these I wonder what I ever really learned in college.)

Sex is a delicate subject and needs to be handled cautiously, even under normal circumstances. Trying to explain it to students whose comprehension was poor was indeed more difficult.

I figured I had two options. The first, and I was strongly leaning in that direction, was to pick up my things and run. Run as fast as I could and never look back. The second was to handle it in the "FBI/CIA" mode: on a need-to-know basis. To me, this was an FBI moment. We spent a little time discussing the difference between girls and boys, then the differences between all of us, ending with things that are unique and special about each person. What began as a lesson in futility actually turned into a lesson in life.

"You know Mr. Yerman," Paul said, as we were walking out to the buses that day. "I'm glad you're my teacher."

It was the first time I had ever heard those words.

"What makes you say that, Paul?"

"You taught me that, no matter what, I'll always have somebody to talk to."

"Thank you, Paul," I said, smiling proudly as he began to climb the stairs to his bus.

"And now I know that girls don't have peters," he said loud enough, I'm sure, for the superintendent to hear.

My smiled turned a little self-conscious as all eyes were upon me, wondering what must have gone on in my room that day.

As I look back on that momentous occasion, I can't help but thank Linda for making my life a little more adventurous. She taught me that the time-out room was not for everyone. I thank Paul for his untainted sincerity as he taught me to deal with problems in an innocent and honest way. I thank both of them for showing me that teaching can, and should, take place anywhere and at any time. Most of all, however, I can't thank them enough for helping me understand that choice number one was never an option.

Chapter Five
We're All Doing the Best We Can

*A*m I a good parent? Who's to say? I like to think I am. I know I've tried to be. I've given my time, support and love to my children. But parenting is not an exact science; far from it! Some people compare parenting to gardening. You plant the seed, feed it, water it, tend it, and when you're finished you have a beautiful flower. Other people see parenting more like a tornado. It jumps out of nowhere without warning. There's no time to understand what is going on while it spins out of control; and once it's over, we assess how much damage has been done. I suspect the answer lies somewhere in the middle, although I have had my share of tornadoes in parenting my kids.

My wife, Deborah, and I have three children, two from my previous marriage and one from hers. Every summer, from the time we merged our families, we would pack up and drive 14 hours to a family cabin in the mountains of North Carolina.

We were married in June and our first trip together was to take place that August. Our children were

between the ages of five and eight. As we wanted everyone to get along, we read some articles and researched
how we might make this happen. (Who were we kidding?) One article, in particular, piqued our interest and
we decided to give it a try.

"What have we got to lose?" we agreed.

Isn't it amazing how statements like this one come
back to bite you in the butt so often in life?

The essence of the article was this: we give each
child ten cents to start. When they act nicely, they get
another nickel. When they misbehave, we take a nickel
back. (Remember, we're talking the early 1980's here; a
nickel went a long way for a kid.) The article promised
that the strategy would not only make a trip pleasant,
but a rewarding adventure, too. It came complete with a
picture of a family just like ours, in a convertible with
the top down, driving in the mountains on a sunny day.
The wind was in their hair, they were all smiling, pointing
and seemingly having a wonderful time.

We packed the kids into our old Volare. It had one
long seat in the back. For those of you without kids, that's
one child on one window, one child on the other window, and one really unhappy kid in the middle, wondering what he did to deserve such punishment. Being
smart parents, we already had that problem covered.
We'd make frequent stops and change the seating
arrangement in the back so that everyone had equal time
in the dreaded abyss that was the middle seat.

We hit our first stumbling block before we even left
the driveway.

"Mom, how come I have to sit in the middle first?"
Ryan said.

"It's because Bryan and Ali are older than you." Deborah answered.

"But that's not fair," he said. "I want to sit by the window first."

Technically we weren't on the road yet, so our nickel plan wasn't in effect. And we certainly didn't have time to debate the word "fair." We didn't know what to do.

Deborah reasoned with Ryan for a long time before resorting to the ultimate parental prerogative.

"Because I said so, that's why!" she boomed as she picked Ryan up and tossed him into the back seat. We were off!

On the road, armed with our nickels, we knew we could make this work. It would have worked, too, if it weren't for three small difficulties: Bryan, Ryan and Alison.

It's just humanly impossible for three children to get along in the back seat of a Volare for 14 hours. Why, you ask? Well, first of all because of the ever-changing enemy camps that formed. A different war broke out every few miles. There were the boys against the girl; Bryan and Ali (my children) against Ryan; the youngest two against the oldest; the oldest two against the youngest, not to mention the individual skirmishes that erupted.

"Mom, she's on my side."

"But honey there is no side. It's all one seat, that'll be a nickel."

"But she's putting her hand near me."

"Alison, keep your hands to yourself. That'll be a nickel."

"Mom, he looked at me."

"Now honey, he's allowed to look at you. That'll be a nickel."

"But he's making faces."

"Ryan, please don't make faces at her. That'll be a nickel."

"Isn't it my turn to sit by the window yet?"

"I'm hungry."

"I'm thirsty."

"I need to go to the bathroom."

"He hit me."

"I did not. I just touched her, like this."

"OW! He hit me again."

It's a 600-mile trip from our house in Florida to North Carolina. We hadn't traveled five miles before our children owed us somewhere in the neighborhood of the gross national product of China.

It got so bad that we found ourselves saying things we swore would never escape from our lips.

"Don't make me stop this car. Do you want me to stop this car? I'm telling you, I will stop this car. I will turn around and take us right back home. Is that what you want?"

After 45 minutes into the trip even the Volare had had enough: it broke down.

The rest I leave to your imagination. I didn't feel or act like a good parent that day. I was tired, frustrated, and confused.

This adventure occurred long after I left Ohio. By then, I had been teaching for years. I was supposed to know a little something about behavior management. Perhaps its purpose was to fortify the Biblical admonition: "Judge not that ye be not judged."

In my early years of teaching I was quick to judge and quick to criticize. I believe it is one of the follies of youth.

Folly or not, it certainly brought me some hard lessons to learn.

Marty was, for me, one of the most sorrowful students I ever had in my class. He spent his day wrapped in a straight jacket, his hands bound behind his back, with a helmet strapped to his head. Whenever his hands were free he would hit his face until he was bleeding everywhere. If his head was free, he would smash it against tables or walls or doors until the blood flowed. Even within the confines of his jacket he was trying to hurt himself in some way. He knew by banging his chin against the table he'd get the bloody results he seemed to crave. I cannot think of a more ghastly sound than the rhythmic thumping of Marty's chin as he beat it against the nearest solid object over and over again, like the drip of an incessant faucet: slow, ceaseless, and pervasive.

When not hunched over, Marty was a tall teenager. It was impossible to determine what he really looked like, as his white skin was a collection of swelling, scars, bruises and open wounds. His red hair was pushed under his helmet, strands peeking out as if trying to escape the abuse.

He'd sit in my classroom, contorted in his straight jacket with a confused forlorn look on his face. I often wondered if his heart was broken. His eyes, always so full of grief, seemed to beg us to help him stop whatever was causing his body to act in this manner. Not a second went by that he wasn't trying to do himself harm. I imagine he even dreamt about hurting himself, although I harbored a secret hope that, perhaps in his dreams, he was pain free and happy.

One of the prevalent theories at that time suggested that people like Marty had so much stimulation going on in their heads that it caused them physical pain. The

self-abuse was their way of trying to cope with the pain.
I had seen people with headaches pound their head in
frustration, why not Marty? Perhaps Marty was just trying
to improve his reception. On the flip side, the theory also
suggested that people like Marty may not feel enough
sensations. His assaults were just his way of bringing feeling into the numbness that was his life. If either portion
of the theory was true, how could I, or anyone, help him?

Marty's mother had an unusual way of coping with
her son's extreme behaviors. She was convinced that
Marty could communicate with her and she took him on
the road to prove this to everyone. She would put a pencil in the portion of his hand that stuck out the back of
the straight jacket. Then she would ask him a question
and, with her hand guiding him, he would write his
answer on a sheet of paper.

The first time I saw this, believe it or not, was on television. She was showing off their unique form of communication. I remember watching it and feeling a
bittersweet mixture of amazement and sadness.

"Hi, Marty," she would say, as she put the pencil into
his hand.

"Hi, Mom," he would write on a tablet she held with
one hand, as she held his writing hand with the other.

"I am only holding his hand to guide him," she would
say. "He's doing the actual writing. Isn't that right, Marty?"

"Yes, Mom," they'd write together.

"Marty, can you tell these nice people where we are
going tomorrow?"

"To the zoo."

"Do you like the zoo?"

"Yes, especially the giraffes."

All the while they were communicating, Marty, who could not see his hand, was trying to bang his chin against his mother's shoulder.

Years later a technique similar to this was discovered called Facilitated Communication. It was met with mixed reviews, as it was difficult to determine who was actually doing the talking. Over the years, I've realized that there are no magic cures, no universal remedies for people with autism. Many techniques come and go. But, if a technique works for even one person, I believe it worthwhile.

I never achieved a modicum of success with Marty. Try as we might, we couldn't get him to stop his incessant self-annihilation. He remained, during my tenure, a sad, self-destructive young man.

Chester, however, was a different story. Chester was a slightly heavy boy, average height, with curly blond hair. He wore a thick pair of dark rimmed glasses and possessed what I have come to know as the autistic smile.

It was very important to Chester's mother that he received a good education. To me, that meant teaching students to grow and become as independent as possible in an accepting and pleasurable environment. To Chester's mother it meant learning reading, writing and arithmetic.

The University School housed the only autistic program in a 50-mile radius, and some of our students traveled a good distance each day. Chester rode the bus for an hour and a half each way. So adamant was Chester's mother about his coming to school that she would drive him to school, in the snow, if the bus couldn't make it.

Many were the snowy winter days when Chester was the only student in my class!

He was a lovely young man, happy, contented. He enjoyed school. His academics were extremely poor, however. He did not recognize the letters of the alphabet or read and his math skills were poor. However, he could print his name, as long as he wrote in BIG letters.

Chester's mother was convinced that he knew more than I was giving him credit for; she positively knew he could read.

"I don't understand what you are saying," she said at a meeting one day. "Chester can read and do simple addition and subtraction. He's just fooling you. If you were a better teacher, you'd know this."

As a first year teacher, and given the "success" I had experienced to date, my confidence was sorely lacking. She could have been right.

"Perhaps," I asked in a shaky voice, "if you'd work with Chester and show me what he can do, I would have a better idea of what you're talking about. If I see what you're doing, then I can repeat it in class."

She agreed and came in armed with a myriad of materials.

As I sat silently, I saw Chester recite his alphabet. It was the ABCs song all school children learn.

Next his mother took out the letter A and showed it to Chester.

"A," he responded.

She showed him the B.

"B," he said.

C, D, E, and on to Z; Chester knew them all.

Chester's mother smiled and stared at me with a look that said, "I told you so."

"Now Chester," she said, "open the book."

Chester complied.

"Now read," she demanded.

Chester began to read.

"The—night—Max—wore—his—wolf—suit..."

As she turned the page, Chester's mother sneered at me again.

Chester and his mother continued through the book without a mistake.

Next it was time for math.

"Chester, what is one plus one?" she asked.

"Two."

"What is one plus two?"

"Three."

On they went until they reached ten. When they had finished, his mother sat tall and reassured in her chair, proud of their mutual accomplishments.

"See," she said. "See, I told you he could do it."

This was a very awkward moment for me. What had I witnessed? Had I seen a boy read who I was convinced could not recognize his alphabet? Or had I seen a young boy with a good memory, who had been drilled repeatedly by his mother, memorize everything she thought she taught him?

Before I passed judgment I had to verify my inclination.

"That was very good, Chester," I said.

"Now, would you mind," I asked his mother, "if I tried something?"

"Not at all," she said confidently.

I took the letters of the alphabet and mixed them up.

"Would you ask Chester what these are now?"

"With pleasure," she said, taking them from my hands. She held up the first letter, a T.

"Chester, what is this letter?"

"A" was his reply.

"No, Chester," she said. "Take a good look at this and tell Mommy what it is."

"B" was his answer.

His mother held up letter after letter. He was unable to recognize any of them.

By the time she got to the tenth letter she was shaking.

"Chester, come on. I know you can do this," she insisted.

"J" Chester insisted, as he began biting his wrist and flapping his hands.

I stopped the lesson.

"But what about the book?" she asked.

I opened the book to the second page and pointed to a word.

"Chester, can you read this word?" I asked.

"The" he said.

I pointed to more words but the results were the same.

Finally, I asked her to give him one of the math problems, out of the order he had learned them.

"No," she said. "What's the point?"

Chester stayed in the classroom with Brenda and the rest of the students while his mother and I went into the observation room.

Chester's mother was a strong-willed, demanding lady. I assumed she was going to let me have it. When we entered the room I was unprepared for her response. She cried.

I found some tissues for her and I talked about Chester. Watching him through the window, I talked about what a nice young man he was and about the things he could do, not what he could not do.

"I'm sorry," I said, when I had finished.

She looked at me through reddened eyes.

"Sorry for what?" she sniffled. "I was so sure you were wrong. I wanted so much to be right."

She began to cry again.

"You have a wonderful son," I said. "Just because he doesn't do these things now doesn't mean he won't or that we'll give up trying. And, while we're at it, we can also work on getting him ready for a job someday. Perhaps we can enjoy him a little bit more."

When I left Kent at the end of the next school year Chester was reading a few safety words, was still printing his name as big as before, and could recognize his coins. There was one significant change, however. His mother thought less about the son she didn't have and seemed much happier with the one she had.

Years later, two separate incidents reminded me of Marty and Chester.

I took my son, Bryan, to get his driver's license. While waiting in line, we observed an older gentleman taking his eye test. He seemed to be having difficulty.

The examiner asked him to read the letters on the first line and he couldn't.

"Are you sure this machine is on?" he asked.

"Yes sir. Please read the first line of letters."

The man looked into the scope.

"You come over here and tell me if you can see anything in this damn machine," he demanded.

With a roll of her eyes, she pivoted the machine around and looked into the lens.

"Yes sir. I can see them."

She repositioned the machine in front of the man.

The man returned his eyes to the machine. This time he was shaking, just like Chester's mom, as he strained to see what he, and the examiner, knew he couldn't.

"Just give me a minute," he said. "I know I'll be able to see them. I know it."

The examiner looked at the man's daughter who had accompanied him to the test. She nodded.

"Come on, Pop," she said. "I'll drive you home."

The old man stood up tall, brushed himself off and took his daughter's arm.

"You know, Pop," his daughter said, as they walked out the door. "This only means we'll get to spend more time together. I can finally repay you for all those years you drove me around."

Amazingly, that same evening, I received a call from Marty's mother. She had also relocated to Florida and somehow found me. She said Marty was still hitting himself, but now lived in an institution. She was able to speak to him on the phone and wanted me to know that he was happier now.

Life is unpredictable. Sometimes just coping with what it throws our way can be a challenge. As much as we hope for something to be different, as much as we will it to change or pray for a miracle, there comes a time when we need to step back, brush ourselves off and accept who we are and the situations life has given us. When we do, we open the door to happiness and peace.

Marty and Chester's mothers made the best of the situation thrust upon them. I believe I initially judged each of them incorrectly. I saw two inflexible, insistent women who would not listen to reason. What I should have seen were two parents with a world of wishes and dreams, each trying to cope with their world as it was falling apart. I should have looked at the journey they were making in life and recognized that they were doing their best to accept a life not of their choosing.

It made a 14-hour trip in a Volare full of kids seem like a walk in the park.

Chapter Six
Dealing with Situations Head-On

Sex! Say the word and a hundred different images pop into a hundred peoples' minds. As a society, we have very mixed reactions to it. Do we talk about it, or not? Do we celebrate it or hide it away in the closet? Most of us (and I use myself only as an example), treat it as we do my crazy Uncle Pete. We all know about him, but no one talks about him. In fact, we hope the subject never comes up. When it does, an awkward, uncomfortable silence is followed by a quick change of conversation.

"Sex? (Silence) Um, yea, sex is something you don't want to do right now. Do you want something to eat? Hey, there's a football game on TV. Is that your mother calling me? Yup, gotta go."

As simple as it seems, sex involves complex feelings and emotions, sound reasoning (OK, sometimes sound reasoning has nothing to do with it), and the ability to share. Our children proceed through the developing years of their lives wondering a lot about sex. Often their questions remain unanswered until experienced, which, if you've ever been there, can be utterly embarrassing.

I'm certain there are parents in the world who discuss sex openly and freely, without reservation. However, I don't think that describes most of us. If we have such a hard time talking about the subject within our own family, how do we handle the subject with children removed from our paternal and maternal instincts, say, with my students for instance?

As we've already seen with little naked Linda, sometimes you have no choice and have to rise (!) to the occasion. So it was with Paul.

Paul was a tall, pudgy 14-year-old, impeccably dressed, with a polite and well-mannered demeanor. He possessed two characteristics that set him apart from the other students in my initial class. The first was that he talked to himself.

Normally, this might not be a problem. Everyone talks to himself at one time or another.

And while I'm on the subject, what is the definition of "normal" anyway? Behavior I consider normal some other person might consider bizarre. As a society, our definition of normal is constantly changing. When *Gone With The Wind* was released, Clark Gable's infamous line, "Frankly, my dear, I don't give a damn" was initially sent to the censors and considered too vulgar for the times. By today's standards, that would rate a PG.

What then is normal behavior? Your guess is as good as mine. We must each set our own standards, based on our upbringing, what we've been taught, and where we are in life at a particular moment. Perhaps abnormal is just normal behavior pushed to an extreme. Take rocking, for instance. Many of us like to gently sway back and forth. This is a normal, relaxing movement. Companies even make furniture to accommodate our inclination. But, if I feel the need to rock violently back and forth in that chair, am I abnormal? Perhaps to some, but I have seen students who view this as perfectly normal behavior.

If I talk to myself, that's normal. If I talked to myself incessantly and to the exclusion of others, that would describe Paul. He kept a running conversation going with himself. He participated in class and did his work. His whispered, one-sided discussions never became an issue, until Mr. Sanderson, a math teacher at the University School, came into my room one day.

"Hey, Jim, you might want to check out the restroom. There's a lot of noise coming from down there."

"Thanks, Mark," I said, heading down the hall toward the restroom.

My students have always been easy targets for ridicule and mockery. I imagined this was another one of those moments, but as I approached the restroom everything seemed calm and relatively quiet. I opened the door to the restroom—still nothing. Then I heard a conversation. It was Paul talking to himself. Wanting to keep Paul's dignity intact, I waited outside the stall and listened. The voice was Paul's, loud and animated, but nothing out of the ordinary. Suddenly I realized he was not alone. There was another distinct voice emanating from the stall.

"Well, it's been nice talking to you," Paul said.

"Thank you," a soprano voice replied.

"Hey, do you know what I think you should do right now?" Paul asked.

"No what?" the high pitched voice retorted.

"I think it's time for you to go back home."

With that, I heard a zip and the toilet flushed.

I must admit, I was bewildered. If I wasn't mistaken I had just heard Paul having a conversation with his penis. How was I to approach this subject? Of course he deserved his privacy, but he was talking to his penis in a public restroom where the acoustics acted like an echo chamber, broadcasting his conversation to anyone in the room. Luckily, today there were no other people there. But someday there would be. I decided to attack the subject head on.

"Paul," I stopped him as he exited the stall, "may I ask what you were doing?"

"Talking to Peter," he said naturally.

I looked around.

"But there is no one else here but you and me, Paul."

"Oh, sure there is." Paul said, unzipping his pants and bringing out his conversation buddy. "This is Peter."

I'm not a puritan, but Paul's "friend" was more than I cared to see. Besides, if anyone else walked into the restroom at that moment it certainly would have looked abnormal. I'd be hard pressed to explain the situation to anyone's satisfaction, even my own.

"Paul, Peter, Jesus, Mary and Joseph!" I stammered, turning away. "Put that thing away."

"Oh, it's OK, Mr. Yerman," Paul reassured me. "Peter's allowed in the restroom."

I had learned how to teach reading, writing and math. I had been shown how to deal with a multitude of specific behaviors. But once again, I was way out of my league. With the emotional well-being of a student in the balance, I knew I needed to move quickly, sternly, yet gently.

I recovered from my initial shock.

"Who told you that?" I implored.

"Mommy and Daddy said that's where Peter had to come out. And you agreed that day on the bus, when I said I'll always have someone to talk to."

"I thought you were talking about me." I said, flabbergasted that I was replaced so easily by a body part.

"Oh, Mr. Yerman. You are so funny," he responded. "Why would I always want to talk to you when I have Peter?"

"Why indeed?" I murmured.

"Paul," I asked as he finally returned Peter to his home, "why do you call it Peter?"

"I remember my mother calling it Peter when I was little. I guess the name just kind of stuck."

"But why do you talk to it?" I asked.

This discussion was not going at all like I had hoped it would.

"Well, I figured if it had a name, I should talk to it. I didn't want it to be lonely."

Perish the thought.

"OK, Paul, but," and here was the $64,000 question, "why does it talk back?"

"Oh, that just started happening one day. I saw my sister, Tammy, playing with her dolls. She would move one to a chair, talk to her, and the doll would talk back. The next time Peter came out, I tried it and he answered me."

"Do you ever talk to Peter when you're not in the restroom?"

"Oh sure. Lot's of times."

"You mean, all those times in class when you're talking to yourself, you're—"

"Talking to Peter? Right." He finished my sentence.

I didn't want to make fun of Paul or hurt his feelings. After all, to him this was perfectly normal. We discussed how a penis was just like any other body part and did not have a name. (I knew this was not a good time to bring up a little known fact that Elvis called his penis "little Elvis." I figured that would only cloud the issue.)

Paul was dejected and confused. He had known Peter much longer than he had known me, and he was certainly more attached to him! So we devised a plan. He would try talking to Peter only at home, when he was alone. He would try to talk to the other students, Brenda or me in school, and if he absolutely had to tell Peter something, he'd whisper it, or better yet, say it only in his head. We both seemed happy with this compromise.

"Now, get back to class," I said, patting him on the back.

I must admit it was a month before I could use the restroom normally. I remained self-conscious for quite a while. I'm not sure if I was afraid I would start talking to my penis, or, God forbid, that it would start talking to me.

Fortunately, my penis never developed a voice and I only encountered this problem once in my teaching career.

I am constantly amazed at life. So many events, some seemingly insignificant, enter our lives and form the foundation of our souls. How these aspects play out says a lot about the type of person we become. An innocent remark by Paul's mom, overheard by a young autistic boy, became a cornerstone for him. He took the information, developed a very honest and, to him, completely normal relationship—one that I dare say no one else in the world would consider normal.

Paul became my teacher that day. If I could have a candid, sincere and dignified conversation with him about his "problem" while it was literally staring me in the face, then I could talk about anything to my students. He helped me see that while it might be uncomfortable, dealing with problems this way is the best solution. He taught me about the ever-changing face of "normal." To him, talking to his penis was as normal as talking to me, even more so.

I haven't seen or heard from Paul in years. But now, when I am around my family and the subject of crazy Uncle Pete comes up, I smile and wonder how the old guy's doing.

Chapter Seven
Don't Jump to Conclusions

⊚

*L*inda had an annoying habit of biting her nails. She didn't just nibble on them. She tore parts of them off and damaged the ends of her fingers. According to Dr. Spock, Anbesol cures young children from sucking their thumb, because the taste is so displeasing.

"I'll give it a try," I said to myself as I laid Dr. Spock's book on the bedside table. "Linda, you've met your match."

I decided to keep a chart to track the rate at which her behavior decreased. Without Anbesol, Linda was biting her fingers at the rate of six times every minute. We devised a procedure: when Linda bit her finger I would say "NO" and put Anbesol on it. When she invariably bit it again the taste would be so offensive she was bound to quit. I stocked up on the remedy, put the chart on the wall and was ready to begin.

Two hours into the procedure I discontinued it. Under the influence of the Anbesol, Linda's biting jumped to 50 times a minute, an increase of 800% of her inappropriate behavior! Apparently neither Dr. Spock nor I anticipated that she might actually enjoy the taste of the liquid! I decided not to give up but to change my treatment. After trying hot mustard (increase of 200%) and extra hot Tabasco sauce (up 500%), I finally gave up in frustration. Linda had won another round. All my preparation and careful planning left me with nothing more than an outrageous supply of Anbesol and a student who was now biting her fingers more than when we started—and smiling at her victory.

Many times the frustration I felt dealing with Linda and other students' behaviors was intense. I'm sure it was no different than the feeling parents experience with raising their children. However, with Linda my frustration was monumental. Many days I felt like screaming, or worse. The trick for me was to back away, reassess, then return with another plan. For Linda's mom, it was a different story.

Linda came into school one day with horrible bruises on her arms and face. The school's procedure for this situation was quite clear. When I saw bruises, I was to tell my superior and he would contact the appropriate agency. Then the agency contacted the parent, in this case, Linda's mom.

Her reaction was confrontational.

She opened my classroom door and yelled at me to come into the hallway. I knew what she wanted and I was ready for her. She was wrong, pure and simple. I was right and nothing she would say would change my mind.

Of course, I was mistaken.

I expected her to be angry with me and was unprepared for what I encountered. She was crying. She told me she had been reprimanded by the agency and asked me why I had called them on her.

"Why didn't you call me first?" she asked.

I hesitated.

My students often stay in my class for many years, so it is imperative that I have a good relationship with their parents. I have always tried to treat my parents like I'd want to be treated by my own children's teachers. Up until that moment, we had had a good relationship.

I explained to her that I had no choice.

She cried again and asked why I didn't at least call her to tell her what I was doing.

"If nothing else, it would have given me a chance to explain," she said.

"What's to explain?" I wondered to myself. "She hit Linda and that's that."

"Yesterday," she began, "Linda was running around the house naked again. I was trying to feed the baby when Linda came into the living room, where we were sitting. She looked at us. I smiled at her, patted the sofa next to me and asked her to sit with us. If I couldn't get her dressed, I figured at least I could get her to sit down. Anyway, she smiled that mischievous smile of hers, darted over to the bookshelf next to us and pulled the entire shelf over. I only had enough time to cover the baby with my body before it hit, or no telling what would have happened. Here, look at this."

She turned and lifted her sweatshirt revealing a huge bruise on her back.

"At this point I lost it," she continued. "I put the baby in her crib, chased Linda, and gave her the beating of her life. Yes, I hit her. But what would you have done?"

With that question lingering in the air, she turned and walked away.

I looked at the ceiling and sighed. I was embarrassed. I guess I didn't have all the answers. Apparently, I didn't have many at all.

I ran down the hall after her. She stopped and turned toward me, still crying.

"I am so sorry," I said. "I didn't realize. I thought I was doing the right thing."

Again I explained to her that I had no choice, but the explanation rang hollow, even to me.

"I promise next time if I have a question, I'll come to you first."

Linda's mom wiped away her tears, gave me a slight smile, then turned and left.

As she walked down the corridor I started thinking about how difficult her job as a parent must be. She was a single mom with three children, one of whom was Linda. I made a pact with myself then and there not to jump to conclusions when it came to the parents of my students. I would try to see all sides of a story before making up my mind.

Linda had bruised her mom's back, but I had bruised her trust and her pride. As she faded from my view, I couldn't help but wonder which one of us had hurt her more.

Chapter Eight

The Thief, A Little Night Music & Fluffy

Dr. Black, a professor from Kent State, was our "resident expert", the person we turned to for advice and guidance. He was constantly sparring with Mr. Mulvaney, our school psychologist and self-proclaimed expert. Each of them continually bombarded us with new ideas and techniques to try with our autistic students.

One day I was told I was getting a new student from Alabama. Generally we don't learn too much about a new student until he or she arrives. Much of the preliminary information I am sent I don't read. Why? Because so many times I receive students with severe problems. I don't want to be prejudiced by another person's analysis. This also helps keep me on my toes and ready for anything.

Mr. Mulvaney delivered the news while Dr. Black and his students were observing.

"Well, Jim, it looks like you'll be getting another student."

"Tomorrow," he added, before I had the chance to ask. I am reasonably sure that Mr. Mulvaney was not completely smitten with my ability after the Bobby episode, and never would be.

"He's been kicked out of every school he's ever been in," he said abruptly.

"Kicked out for what?" I asked.

"Not sure. Seems he's a bit of a behavior problem."

"Gee, Mr. Mulvaney. We're going to the baseball game tomorrow. (For weeks my class had been scheduled for an outing at a local stadium to watch a game.) Do you think we should take him?"

"Ronald, his name's Ronald. You either take him with you or cancel the trip."

It was a statement not unlike, "Do you want the shot in your arm or your butt?"

"Dr. Black, what do you think?" I asked, hoping the two of them could agree on something.

"Well, we typically don't see many bizarre behaviors the first day in a new program. It's called the honeymoon period. I don't think there'll be a problem."

"Good, its settled then," Mr. Mulvaney stated. "Have fun." And he was out the door.

Ronald was a very verbal, social, polite and talkative young man. He was five feet tall and very skinny; he couldn't have weighed more than 75 pounds. He had a full head of blond hair and wore glasses that were supposed to help correct his vision, as his eyes pointed in two different directions. It was as if they worked independently of each other. One looked straight ahead; the other off to the left. He could read, but had to be close to the material and would turn his head back and forth, like adjusting the lens on binoculars, until he was focused.

He also walked a little bent over from a permanent arch in his back and talked with a pronounced southern drawl. Every word he uttered was long and drawn out.

He seemed very pleasant as we departed school and headed for the game. At the time, in fact, I remember wondering why he was ever placed in my class in the first place. Other than his eyes and awkward gait, he seemed pretty normal. He was able to converse with me and seemed to take an instant liking to Brenda.

We were ushered into our seats and settled down to watch the game.

I'm not sure at what exact moment I realized the honeymoon was over with Ronald. Perhaps it was the first time he laughed; it was very sinister. Or perhaps it was when he looked at me. He would peer at me over the top of his glasses, his mouth opened slightly. He would snicker while his head bobbed up and down. The asymmetry of his eyes gave them a sneaky, almost cunning quality. Or perhaps it was when, out of the blue, as we were sitting watching the game, he leaned over and tapped the lady in front of me on the shoulder.

"Excuse me, ma'am," he said, in his most cordial southern accent. "You see this man over here?"

He was pointing to me.

The lady looked at me and I smiled, albeit a confused, halfhearted smile.

"This man's a thief," Ronald continued.

I didn't have time to react before he dropped the second bomb.

"He stole me from my father. He's a dirty rotten thief."

I was beginning to see why Ronald's tenure at his previous schools ended so quickly.

"Ya gotta help me, ma'am," he continued. "He said if I tell anyone he's gonna kill me. You don't want him to kill me, do you?"

The lady looked at me with disdain.

I shrugged my shoulders and apologized. What else could I do? I only hoped she didn't believe his story.

"Don't let him get away with this, please."

The lady got up and abruptly changed her seat.

When he realized his damsel was not distressed, he stopped.

"Thank goodness." I sighed to myself.

Apparently not only was the honeymoon over but Ronald was working on the divorce.

He stood up and pointed at me.

"This man's a thief," he screamed. "He's a thief. If someone doesn't stop him he's gonna kill me. He's—"

Without further ado, I picked Ronald up and headed for the exit. Unfortunately, this only made his story more believable.

"You see, you see," he screamed, as he kicked and hit me with his hands. "He's gonna take me outside and he's gonna kill me. Help!"

With that an usher blocked our way. It seemed to me that no one was watching the game anymore. There was a better show in the stands.

"May I ask where you're going?" the usher queried.

This was just getting better and better. I had to explain to a man I didn't know that a student I didn't know was saying things I didn't understand for reasons I also didn't know. I was having trouble believing this myself. I explained the circumstances as best I could and, mercifully, the usher acquiesced. I took Ronald outside.

As soon as we exited the gate Ronald began bobbing up and down, slapping his legs and laughing.

"I guess I really got you, didn't I, Mr. Yerman?"

"Yes, Ronald," I said. "I guess you did. But why?" I asked.

"Because it's funny," he answered.

Next he began an unusual behavior that I would come to know as his victory dance. He stood with one foot in front of the other, rocking back and forth while flapping his arms out to the side.

I missed the rest of the game as I was treated to many encore performances of "This man's a thief." As we waited on a bench outside the stadium, Ronald practiced his routine on anybody and everybody who passed by. Old or young, big or little, male or female, all were politely interrupted, then told the story of the thief and the killing to be. I endured his behavior in much the same way a parent endures his child acting up in public. I smiled, apologized, and as Ronald continued performing his victory dance, planned my revenge.

The next day, as Ronald was settling into his routine, we were scheduled to try something new with Linda.

Dr. Black had read encouraging studies about the use of classical music with autistic students. He suggested I try out some soothing classical music to help settle Linda down. I reminded him of the Rossini strip tease, but he was undeterred.

We chose Mozart. I sat Linda across from me and set the record player in the middle of the table. She watched me closely as she always did. She needed to know her enemy to plan her attack. I cued up "A Little Night Music." She cocked her head and continued watching me. I smiled at her as I listened to the music, hoping she was listening, too. Then she smiled.

"Ah," I said to myself, "it's working."

Dr. Black, who was observing with his students, must have been pleased.

I began to work with Linda, trying to get her to say "Mama." I had heard her say the sounds on her own. I was now trying to attach them to a picture of her mom.

Linda watched me intently. Perhaps we were experiencing a breakthrough.

Slowly Linda rose. She looked at me. I smiled. She smiled; so far so good. Next she walked over to the record player and watched the record spinning around. Again she looked at me, then raised her finger to her glasses and smiled.

"This can't be good," I muttered to myself.

Before I could say "epiphany" she picked up the record player and tossed it across the room. I looked at the pile of electrical parts that once was the record player, then back at Linda. She was smiling and biting her fingers. I believe this was her way of telling me that Mozart's "Night Music" and the experiment were officially over.

I've often wondered if it was Mozart, or classical music in general that she didn't like, but I never found out. Our budget didn't allow for any more experimentation.

That's not quite true. Experimentation was encouraged. Buying new record players was not.

Not long after this musical disaster a woman from Kent, Mrs. Smythe, approached me with another idea. She had read about a program where animals were brought into nursing homes to help the patients. According to the article, the patients and animals formed relationships that were mutually beneficial. The elderly patients were happy and excited to see these animals each week, and the animals received a little extra loving.

It was Mrs. Smythe's idea to give my students the same experience.

"Who knows what good things might happen," she said enthusiastically to Dr. Black, Mr. Mulvaney and my students' parents, all gathered to discuss her proposal. "If the students are afraid we won't force them to do anything. Besides, what's the worse that could happen? A puppy may lick them or it'll jump in their laps? Let's wait and see. It could be wonderful."

Everyone agreed and it was arranged.

On the scheduled day Mrs. Smythe introduced Fluffy to the class. Fluffy was a miniature French Poodle with curly white hair, just like her name. She looked like a little white cloud cuddled in Mrs. Smythe's arms. Mrs. Smythe was a real trouper. She patiently took Fluffy around to each of my students and gave them a chance to touch her. The reactions were mixed, from turning away, to a quick jab, to a soft stroke. Randy even held her cautiously, like a father cradling a newborn.

"This is going great," I said to Mrs. Smythe.

She smiled and nodded.

Ronald's reaction was disconcerting.

"You know, I had a dog like this once," he said, while petting Fluffy.

"Oh, you did?" Mrs. Smythe said. "Where is he now?"

"We ate him," he said, preparing to do his victory dance.

Mrs. Smythe was shocked, quickly pulling Fluffy away from Ronald for protection.

"Oh, that Ronald, such a kidder," I said.

"Do you think I should put him down?" Mrs. Smythe asked, after recovering from the mental picture of her little Fluffy cooking in a pot.

"Sure," I said naively.

She placed Fluffy on the floor and the little pooch played at the feet of my students. Fluffy made the rounds to my students, instinctively staying away from Ronald. She would, as puppies are wont to do, spring up and down at their feet.

It was here that the trouble started. Mrs. Smythe and I saw Fluffy as a soft, cute, cuddly member of the animal kingdom. Where we saw Fluffy as a possible bridge out of my students' autism, apparently Linda was beginning to see her as a nuisance. Where my students, excluding Ronald, saw Fluffy as something to touch, play with, pet, and experience, Linda was seeing her as a ball with fur.

Just as Mrs. Smythe and I were congratulating ourselves on a successful experiment, I looked over at Linda. Tiring of Fluffy's incessant perkiness, Linda seized the dog by the neck. Everything began to move in slow motion.

"LINDA!" I screamed. "NO!"

But it was too late.

As I started across the room toward her desk I got a quick glimpse of Fluffy. Her little mouth was wide open and her cute little eyes were swept with fear.

The next thing I knew, Fluffy was flying. As she floated across the classroom, she really did look like a soft fluffy cloud. Until that is, she smacked into the wall.

It was like something out of the Saturday morning cartoons. Her furry little paws were stretched out to her sides as she hit. She seemed to stay suspended on the wall for a few seconds before slowly sliding to the floor.

"Oh, Fluffy," Mrs. Smythe said, as we reached her capsized puppy. "Fluffy, are you all right?"

She picked up her little dog. He was dazed but unharmed.

I apologized profusely to Mrs. Smythe as she scooped him up and rushed out the door, never to return again.

Ronald couldn't resist. "I told you we should've eaten that little dog."

It didn't take us long to understand that our "experts" knew about as much as we did about teaching students with autism, and sometimes, even less.

Ronald, Linda, Anbesol, Mozart, Fluffy—so much of what we do in life is trial and error. I still hold fast to the belief that taking risks, trying new ideas and experimentation is the correct approach to teaching. No amount of college education or textbooks can possibly prepare us for the experiences that lie ahead. Life offers no absolutes and the best we can do is accept our limitations, be flexible enough to change, and persistent enough to keep trying.

We never know which new idea or experiment will be the one that makes a difference. Perhaps the very next new idea we try with Linda will get through to her.

I often think about this as I watch the clouds roll by on a beautiful day. Without fail, I catch a glimpse of a cloud with that familiar Fluffy shape, and, I wonder. With a little more persistence and luck, perhaps it would have been Linda, instead of Fluffy, who soared that day.

Chapter Nine
Sometimes You Just Get Lucky

@

*T*he other characteristic that set Paul apart from the rest of my students (the first being his conversations with Peter) concerned feet, or to be more exact, shoes. He had an unusually intense interest in them. He'd bring in shoe catalogues to peruse and his favorite album was the Partridge Family, with David Cassidy on the cover in his bare feet. He knew everything there was to know about shoes. He could look at your shoes and tell you what style you were wearing, out of what material they were manufactured and by whom.

I hadn't had to deal with fetishes before. Summoning all my extensive knowledge and maturity, I made the decision to ignore it, in hopes it would go away. Actually, Paul treated shoes more like a "hobby"; it seemed harmless enough.

Dr. Clark, a professor at Kent State, taught economics at the University School. He was in his mid 50's with white hair and a neatly trimmed silver beard and mustache. He wore sporty glasses, dressed only in the finest clothes and always wore a pair of white shoes.

Paul made friends with Dr. Clark instantly. When they passed in the hall, Paul would say hello and Dr. Clark would return the greeting. Paul would always comment on the professor's shoes and the professor took these compliments in stride.

The more I watched Paul and the professor, however, the more concerned I became with Paul's obsession. It quickly became evident to me that the fetish needed to be discouraged. I asked Paul to give up talking to Dr. Clark about his feet and together, we devised other questions he could pose to the professor. He agreed.

When I approached Dr. Clark about Paul's shoe fetish he disagreed with me. He said I was making a mountain out of a molehill. He was sure Paul meant him no harm and knew he was much too polite and naíve to have a sexual attraction to his shoes or anyone else's, for that matter. Since he had been teaching for 15 years and this was only my second, he was sure he knew how to handle the situation. I apologized, retreated, and hoped he was right.

It was early the next month when the professor stuck his head in my doorway, his face as white as his hair.

"Professor Clark," I exclaimed, "is everything all right?"

"He humped my feet," he mumbled. "He humped my feet."

I looked around the room. Paul had not yet returned from the restroom.

I made a mild attempt at consoling Dr. Clark, but Paul was my main concern. Besides, the good professor had been teaching for 15 years; he could handle it. I let Brenda know what had happened then ran to the restroom. It was empty except for Paul and Peter, so I listened.

"Oh Paul, how could you be so stupid?" came the high pitched question.

It seems I was thinking along the same lines as Paul's penis.

"I'm so sorry. I was coming back from the restroom when Professor Clark asked how I was doing. I know I'm not supposed to talk about his shoes, so I said fine. Then Professor Clark asked me about my new shoes. He said they were very nice. I thanked him for noticing them. I said how wonderful I thought his were, that he wore the nicest shoes in the whole school and you know what he said?"

"No, what?" I whispered in tandem with his penis.

"He said thanks and said I could take a closer look if I'd like."

I shuddered in disgust, not at Paul, but at Professor Clark's total disregard for my warning.

"Sure," I said, bending down to take a look. "They were white Oxfords, polished and clean. I ran my hand along the smooth leather. It felt so wonderful. Then, before I knew it, I was on top of them, Professor Clark was screaming and I ran in here to hide."

I waited, trying to think of something appropriate to say. I wanted to tell Paul it wasn't entirely his fault, although his actions were wrong. I wanted to tell him how Dr. Clark got just what he deserved. But I couldn't find the right words, so I said nothing.

"You need to apologize to Dr. Clark," Peter said. "Tell him you are sorry and it will never happen again."

"Yes, you're right," Paul agreed.

I heard his zipper close and left the restroom before he noticed me.

I was standing in the hall when Paul came out.

"Mr. Yerman," he said, before I had a chance to speak, "I'm sorry."

"No, it's me who is sorry."

Paul and I turned around to see Professor Clark.

"Paul, I am sorry," he repeated. Then he looked at me. "I should have realized. I'm sorry I put you in that position. Please forgive me."

"I'm sorry too, Professor Clark," Paul said.

The professor extended his hand and Paul shook it.

"May I walk you back to your room?" he asked.

Paul looked at me.

I smiled.

"Sure," he said.

I lingered as Dr. Clark escorted Paul back to the room. Along the way the professor looked over his shoulder at me, and smiled.

I nodded and smiled back.

Quite a bit had occurred in those last few minutes. I had been told that one of my students masturbated on the shoes of an Economics professor. I had listened in a restroom while the young man's penis gave him better advice than I could. I had watched that professor, who had declined greatly in my admiration, handle the situation with dignity while retaining his and my student's self-respect. All this had happened while I stood there with my mouth open, watching.

None of us mentioned the incident again, but each of us learned something. Paul now understood that discretion was the better part of valor. The professor believed anything I told him. I realized that I didn't have to find a solution to every problem. Sometimes they just work themselves out.

Other times, however, you need a little luck.

The more we got to know Ronald, the more bizarre he became. He loved to intimidate my students.

He would walk up to Russell and look him right in the eyes.

"Russell, I'm gonna kill you," he'd say, with his accent in full drawl.

"You know I can do it. I'm gonna take you outside and I'm gonna kill you. Kill you dead. Maybe I'll cut you. Yea, maybe I'll get my daddy's knife and cut you up."

Poor Russell; if he didn't have underwear on his head someone was threatening to cut him into pieces.

Since Ronald became part of my classroom, I had been trying to deal with him on a higher plane. I talked to him about respecting other people and doing the right thing. I felt he could handle the complexities of the situation. Nothing I said, however, curbed his roguish disobedience.

As I followed Paul back to the room that day all was silent. I wasn't sure what the other students had heard. I had hoped to gloss over Paul's situation and return to work. Of course, these hopes were dashed instantly.

"So Paul," Ronald drawled as he prepared to go into his victory dance. "Hump any good shoes lately?"

This was the last straw. He had finally gone too far.

I walked over to his desk, told him we had had enough of his mouth, and marched him into the time-out room.

His reaction was unexpected.

He had taken an instant liking to Brenda but refused to call her by that name, preferring Barbara. I think he liked the sound "Barbara" made. Or, it was just another way of antagonizing us.

Once in the time-out room he began pleading to Brenda.

"Oh Barbara, please don't let him do this to me. Barbara, Barbara, I thought you loved me. Barbara, won't you help me? Please, Barbara. Barbara, don't let this man kill me." He wailed on and on.

We could see one of his eyes pushed against one of the holes in the time-out room.

After his five minutes elapsed I brought him back to his seat.

"That was mean, Mr. Yerman, just plain mean."

Then he looked at Brenda.

"And Barbara," he said shaking his head. "Barbara, you hurt me. You hurt me real bad."

Then he put his head down on his desk and began to cry.

"I hated it, Mr. Yerman. Please don't put me in there again," he implored.

"Then," I said getting right in his face, "you'd better behave yourself, Ronald."

And he did. In fact, that was the last time we had any trouble with him. He turned into the polite young man he had pretended to be all this time, until he moved back to Alabama a few weeks before the end of the school year.

Nowadays when I hear a high pitched sound similar to Peter's or that peculiar southern drawl of Ronald's, I look around to see if they're nearby. Of course, they're not.

For a brief yet intense time they were part of my life. When I am reminded of them, as I often am, I miss them. I wonder what Peter's up to these days and I shudder to think of what Ronald might have in store for me.

I never took the opportunity to thank them for the growth, the laughter, and the challenges they bestowed upon me. It's something I didn't think of at the time. Now we've each moved on with our lives, the time has passed and it's too late.

Or maybe not. Thanks, you guys!

Chapter Ten
Hello & Goodbye

I loved Linda and the challenge of working with her. Unfortunately, Mr. Mulvaney felt the opposite. He preferred my students to be autistic but look and act normally. Linda was too bizarre and had too many strange behaviors for him and she wasn't good for public relations. He wanted her out of the program; I didn't. We constantly butted heads on the subject.

I had been trying all year to teach her to say "mama." Actually, I had heard her say it many times to herself, but she didn't associate the meaning of the word. Nothing came easy with Linda. I would say "mama" and eat a variety of foods, from cookies to nuts, then try to elicit the same word from Linda while showing her a picture of her mom. I had been working on this daily for seven months without gaining anything except weight. One day I tried M & M's.

"Linda, look at this," I said, showing her a picture of her mom. "Mama," I said, then popped an M & M in my mouth.

"Who is this, Linda?" I asked, showing her the picture.

"Mama," came her unexpected reply.

When you've been waiting for something for a long time and it finally happens, a strange reaction occurs—you don't believe it. I remember looking around the room to see if someone else had said it.

Tentatively, I tried again.

I held up the picture and asked, "Who's this, Linda?"

"Mama," she said.

I looked at her. She was smiling. For once that smile didn't mean she'd beaten me. This time it meant we had won together.

I called Brenda over to make sure I wasn't going crazy.

"Mama," she said.

We were ecstatic. We hugged her and each other and anyone else who was in the vicinity.

"Mama!" Isn't it amazing the little things in life that can give us such pleasure?

I was tempted to call her mom, but decided to surprise her. As the time for her to pick up Linda neared, I became anxious. Linda had been saying "mama" all day but I wasn't sure what she would do in front of her mom. Would she be able to make the connection that this was her mom? Or, would she run past her and out to the car as usual?

"She's coming," Brenda announced. "She's coming."

I ran over to Linda.

"Linda, your mama's coming. Mama, mama, mama." At least I was sure I could say it.

When her mom entered the room I motioned her over to Linda's desk.

"Linda, look who's here," I said. "It's Mama. Who's this?"

Linda looked over at her mother, glanced back to me and smiled.

"Mama," she said smiling.

"Who's this Linda?" I asked again.

"Mama," she repeated.

I looked up at Linda's mom and smiled. She stood there in disbelief.

I repeated the question and Linda repeated her response.

I looked at Linda's mom again and nodded my head in encouragement. She looked deeply into my eyes, then into Linda's, who was sitting as straight as she could sit and smiling. Then she touched my shoulder, covered her mouth and began to cry.

She scooped Linda up and hugged her.

"Mama," Linda said.

Linda's mom embraced her for a long time and listened to the "mama" refrain over and over again. Her eyes were closed and I could only wonder what she must have been feeling. Finally she opened her eyes and while still caressing her daughter, smiled at me.

Not a word was spoken between us. Yet I could feel her satisfaction fill me as Linda and her mom waltzed out of the room.

Shortly thereafter Mr. Mulvaney devised a plan to remove Linda from the program. He could only see her as the uncontrollable child who ran naked through the halls and threw record players and dogs. He never took the time to appreciate the unique little girl we had come to love. Buoyed by the fact she had just spoken her first word and the infinite possibilities that lay ahead, I was determined to keep her in my class.

Because he was the school psychologist, Mr. Mulvaney decided he would test Linda to see if she belonged in the class. I met with him prior to the testing with my concerns. I knew what Linda could do; the test would only prove what she couldn't do. It would be a worthless undertaking. What I failed to realize was that Mr. Mulvaney was counting on that.

On testing day he came armed with his test and a pound of M & M's. Figuring Linda needed an ally, I asked if I could accompany her.

"I can handle it just fine, thank you," he said, declining my request.

They entered the observation room and within two minutes Linda had thrown his beloved test across the room, pages flying in every direction. One minute later Mr. Mulvaney emerged from the room, a piece of his test in each hand and M & M's smeared all over his white shirt and tie. I couldn't make out what he was mumbling as he walked away, but it served him right. He got just what he deserved.

Unfortunately, he would have the last laugh. One week later he came to my room to inform me that Linda was being expelled from the program. She would be allowed to remain until the end of the year, exactly two weeks away, but then she was out.

I pleaded with him to change his mind.

"My God, Mr. Mulvaney," I said. "We were just beginning to make some real progress. Please don't do this. Besides, where will she go?"

"That's not my problem," he said, turning to walk away. "And, it's no longer your problem either."

The next two weeks were difficult, at best, as we waited for the dreaded day to arrive. I don't think Linda knew what was happening. I know she didn't understand that, when we said good-bye that last day, we would never see each other again. I gave her a big hug. She looked at me and smiled. As she walked away holding her mother's hand, she looked back over her shoulder and waved.

"Ba," she said for the first time. "Ba."

The following day I quit. I handed in my resignation and said "ba" to the Kent City Schools, closing a wonderful chapter in my life.

It has been many years since saying good-bye to Linda. I have taught many other children since then. At times, though, I catch myself wondering about her. I think of her head turned slightly to one side, her glasses crooked across her face and her wonderful smile. I see her naked little butt running down the halls of the University School and I wonder if she ever thinks of me. Perhaps she can't listen to classical music, or use Tabasco sauce, or eat M & M's without smiling. I know I can't.

Chapter Eleven
Thank God for Do-overs

❦

"*P*atient" is an interesting word. It means the ability to tolerate annoyances without complaint or anger, to stay calm and accepting under difficult circumstances, to remain cool under fire. Yet there is something dichotomous about it. A patient person who suppresses his emotions could develop an ulcer and end up in the hospital as a patient. The same quality that most people assume is a positive trait, the ability to tolerate adversity, can itself lead to adversity.

This word has always intrigued me. It's often assumed, given what I do, that I embody its definition.

"Oh, you must have so much patience to work with these children."

"You need to have a lot of patience, don't you?"

"I don't think I have the patience to do what you do."

"You must be very patient."

I've heard how patient I am so many times that I often want to grab the next person that mentions the word and ring his ever-loving neck. How's that for patience!

The fact is I am extremely impatient with certain aspects of my students' behaviors, those that have nothing to do with their autism. I expect my students to follow the same guidelines we all follow in a polite society and I am impatient when they do not. I teach 14-22 year old students who, when they leave my program, need to be prepared for the rest of their lives. I haven't the time to be patient.

Yet, I am very patient with the effects of autism over which they have no control.

When I played little league baseball I wasn't the best player on the team. I played right field. In little league you didn't try out for right field, you were relegated to it. It was the spot reserved for the player who was not to touch the ball under any circumstances. Right field was far enough away that in most games a ball never got out there, but it was close enough that coach could make sure my parents were happy.

"Isn't that Jim out there in right field?" my unsuspecting dad would ask my equally clueless mom.

"Yes, it is!" she'd say. "He must be pretty good, because the other team is afraid to hit any balls his way."

Suffice it to say my baseball talents were limited. During practice, when the coach would hit me a ball and I'd drop it, as I often did, or when I'd swing and miss a pitch, he'd give me a do-over. I accumulated so many do-overs that it became my nickname.

"Hey Do-Over, throw me the ball."

"Come on, Do-Over, you can do it."

That year coach had surprised us by having our nicknames emblazoned across the back of our new uniforms. There was Slugger, Sparky, Jimbo, and mine: Doover.

That's right, mine said Doover. Apparently the uniform company missed the space between the two words and thought Doover was my nickname. How humiliating! Even my jersey was a do-over. To add insult to injury, my new nickname caught on and for the rest of my little league tenure (which mercifully was not long), I was known as the Doover.

I keep this part of my life in mind when I'm teaching my students with autism. Their inability to learn is not meant to hurt me. When they fail to grasp certain concepts it's not because of a lack of desire. They want to learn, as much as I wanted to catch and hit. They just need an abundance of do-overs to help them. And who better to see that they get them than the Doover himself?

Ironically, the whole do-over scenario was running through my mind as I was driving from Ohio, (remember I had just quit my job) to Florida, where I was hoping to find one. Maggie had moved to Florida a year earlier. Encouraged by her optimism that I could obtain employment there, we followed her to the Sunshine State. If I had kept my little league jersey I would have been wearing it that day, because we were in the midst of the ultimate do-over.

Maggie was right. I quickly found a job in the Pinellas County School system teaching an autistic class. When they heard I had experience they hired me on the spot. In 1978 there weren't a lot of teachers with experience in autism, which meant the interview process was rather short.

"Mr. Yerman, I see you've taught autistic students in Ohio. Is that true?"

"Yes, I have been teaching in—"

"When can you start?"

I often thought if Captain Kangaroo had shown up and said he had experience with autism he would have been hired too. No matter, I had a job at Nina Harris, a center housing only handicapped students. I would be teaching one of two autistic classes in the school. I was delighted.

Maggie was now teaching regular elementary students. As fate would have it though, another woman teacher taught the autistic class next to mine. Her name was Nancy. Like Maggie before her, she helped me get started and we soon became good friends. Nancy was around that first day, my formal initiation to teaching in Florida.

Susan was a student in my first class at Nina. She was non-verbal, had wavy black shoulder length hair, big green eyes, chubby cheeks and a beautiful smile. The only sounds she made came from the grinding of her teeth or an occasional grunt. She was a petite girl who was very autistic, shutting out the rest of the world and preferring to play with strings or spin objects. She was particularly adept at spinning. Susan would get an object spinning, watch as it continued spinning on its own, then put her arms out and begin flapping and swirling them faster and faster. It was as if she became part of the spinning. The happiest I ever saw her was when she was experiencing this mutual spin.

Until one day, that is when something more interesting caught her eye. After I had been teaching for a couple of months, I bent down to say hello to Susan. She smiled and shook her hands at me. I wasn't sure what she wanted so I leaned closer. Suddenly she gave me a big hug. I was ecstatic! Susan did not like being held by any-one. I picked her up and she continued to hug me. I carried her around spinning and dancing as she kept hugging my neck. I called Dolly, my assistant, and she clapped her hands in amazement. We called to Nancy, who also beamed with excitement.

"Do you think this is some kind of breakthrough?" I asked Nancy.

She smiled, then began to laugh.

"Jim," she said.

"You know, I think I'll carry Susan down to the office and show Dr. Higgins," I said. Dr. Higgins was the principal.

"Jim," Nancy repeated.

"Could you cover my class for me?"

"Sure Jim, but—"

"Maybe I'll call her mom, too."

"JIM!" Nancy yelled, momentarily interrupting my euphoria.

I stopped and turned toward her.

"Jim, before you go," Nancy said between pants of laughter, "I think there's something you should know."

"What's that?"

"Well, Dr. Freud, you may want to check out your shirt first."

"My shirt? What's wrong with my shirt?"

"Take a look at your sleeve."

Awkwardly I turned my head to look at my sleeve, partially hidden by Susan's head. It seemed that when I first bent over to Susan she noticed a loose string on my sleeve. As I watched she was pulling that errant string as fast as her little hands could move. As she pulled, my sleeve was unraveling at record speed. She was amazing; her little hands were a blur and the faster she worked the less sleeve remained. She was like a spider deconstructing a web.

"Susan," I said angrily, pulling her off my sleeve and setting her back on the floor, "stop that."

There I stood, a picture of fashion, wearing a shirt with one good sleeve and the other, a tangled ball hanging by a thread. Susan began to cry and wave her arms at me as she had before. I surmised she wouldn't be happy until I was topless.

By this time Nancy was having trouble staying upright, she was laughing so hard.

I brushed myself off, trying in vain to gather any shred of self-respect, made all the more difficult by my tattered clothing.

"Thanks Nancy," I said. "I think I can handle it from here."

Nancy said not a word; she still hadn't caught her breath from all her laughing. She nodded, waved, and left my room.

I looked at Susan crying on the floor and frantically waving at the remnants of what was my sleeve.

I walked over to my desk.

"Come here, Susan," I said.

She ran over to me.

I took out a pair of scissors, cut the string that was holding the giant ball of thread and handed it to Susan. After all her hard work I figured she deserved it.

She grabbed her prize, began laughing, and ran to the other side of the room to twirl it.

"Welcome to Florida," Nancy said, poking her head back in the room.

"Thanks," I said as I watched Susan happily twirl her reward.

I spent the rest of that day either fielding teacher's congratulations on my breakthrough, as the story spread, or explaining to the uninformed what kind of fashion statement I was trying to make.

"I had two sleeves this morning," I'd say, "but it's a long story. Go ask Nancy; I'm sure she'd be delighted to tell you."

My first encounter with Ethan, another student in my class at Nina, was somewhat more positive. More than a few teachers came to me with the complaint that Ethan drove them crazy. He cried and moaned throughout the day and his persistent whimpering was a constant annoyance.

"All he does is cry," was their universal comment. "He's going to drive you insane."

Ethan was a thin, nine-year-old boy with light hair, pale skin and rosy cheeks. In addition to autism, he suffered from muscular dystrophy, a progressive muscle disorder marked by a gradual wasting of skeletal muscle. When I first saw him he was still able to walk, albeit very slowly and on his tiptoes. Eventually he would be confined to a wheel chair as his condition progressed. Perhaps he had good reasons to cry and moan. He was slowly dying. And, cry and moan he did. Despite his muscular dystrophy he didn't seem to be in any pain, at least none he could verbalize. His only communication was his crying and it was constant.

I decided to do a little investigating and read his file, which went against a general rule of mine at the time. I took out his latest psychological evaluation, completed the year before. Psychological evaluations are done periodically to evaluate progress and determine placement. They are good indicators of progress for many people, but I've never had much faith in them with regard to my low-functioning students (remember Linda?).

Ethan's test contained some very interesting information. The psychologist didn't have much luck testing him. He wrote that Ethan did quite a bit of crying and didn't answer many questions. However, the next sentence jumped off the page like a character in a 3-D movie. On a particular portion of the test Ethan was to point to objects as a way of showing his comprehension. The psychologist, who had difficulty eliciting Ethan's cooperation, wrote the following preposterous statement:

Told Ethan to point to the house. He ignored me and wrote the word house instead. IQ-40.

Attached to the test was a sample of Ethan's work; on the paper he had written h-o-u-s-e. Yes, he had ignored the psychologist's directions but he had correctly written the word he was supposed to point out. How could he have had an IQ of 40 and spell the word "house" correctly? The answer was simple: he couldn't. There was more to Ethan than his crying and moaning.

Since he could spell one word, I reasoned he could spell others. I equipped him with a pad of paper and a pencil, hoping he would begin using them as a means of communication. If he was thirsty, I instructed him to write "water." If he needed the restroom, I asked him to write it. This primitive system worked like a dream and Ethan began communicating with us!

Sadly, his muscular dystrophy soon robbed him of his ability to write. We set him up with an electric typewriter and he was off and typing with ease. We all loved the communication (I still have the typewriter in my room today). As the muscular dystrophy continued its sinister advance through his body and he lost the use of his arms, Ethan was equipped with metal braces that attached to his wheelchair. These braces would pivot easily allowing him to move his hands into the position he needed to type. His fingers would walk over the keys as he strained to find the correct letters. His spelling deteriorated as he lost control of his limbs, but his writing still made sense to us and he still loved it. I have a cherished memory of Ethan, attached to his apparatus, smiling and surveying his keys as he typed his messages to us.

Susan and Ethan's stories are joined by a universal bond of hope.

Unlike many other people, I didn't give up hope on Ethan. I was lucky enough to give him a do-over and he sparkled. Although he didn't begin writing manuscripts, or even stop his whining and crying entirely, he did live a more productive and happy life. He participated a little more, laughed a little more and seemed to enjoy life a little more. We should all be so lucky.

Susan's breakthrough was a blunder born out of hope. I sometimes wonder if the parents of my students hope that today will be the day their son or daughter "wakes up" from their autism? What an easy trap that is to fall into. No matter how many years I teach, no matter how much I understand my students and accept them for who they are, I will never stop looking for a key that will bring them out of the world they inhabit. Susan showed me that hope swings on a tenuous string, but no matter how tenuous, we need to hold on to it.

I have been very lucky in my life. I am healthy, happily married and have a wonderful family life, filled with love and merriment. It is the source of my patience. Yet, I work every day with students who don't speak, have trouble thinking, have seizures, exhibit bizarre behaviors and will probably never find the level of enjoyment and fulfillment in their lives that I have found in mine. They struggle daily in this confusing world. So do their parents, as they cope with shattered dreams and anxiety about the future. They are the source of my hope and understanding.

Patience, hope and understanding do not always lead to success. But in the face of defeat, there's always a do-over just around the corner.

Chapter Twelve

Seeing the World through Rose-colored Glasses

*C*radling a newborn baby in your arms, seconds after he enters the world. Peering out early one morning to find the landscape covered in a soft ivory blanket of snow. Watching the red-hot orange sun as it slowly sinks into the ocean. Looking skyward on an ebony night at a never-ending expanse of twinkling stars. There are moments in our lives that are forever etched in our minds. They fill us with wonder and replenish our soul.

Much of what we do in life is predictable. We eat, work, play, and sleep. Immersed in the mundane, our vision frequently becomes clouded to the wonders encircling us. Perhaps that's why we store these precious memories away so that, at the end of a long day, we can remember a moment that transcends the ordinary, if only for an instant.

I deal with students whose development, by definition, is slow. This compels me to look at life through a different set of lenses, to slow down and watch for little snippets of progress, little glimmers of hope. However, in doing so, I become privy to many of life's miracles that other people are too busy to notice.

One such marvel is language. Its emergence is both wondrous and beautiful. Our mastery of it determines much about our quality of life. It is the bridge for connecting with the rest of the world and becomes a cornerstone of our existence.

Being aware of its wonder is simple; understanding it is much more complicated.

Take a baby, for instance. His first form of communication is a gesture and gestures, from the onset, are ambiguous. Swayed by the pride of a new father, when my son smiled at me for the first time I read his gesture as a sign that he was recognizing me as his dad. It communicated his happiness and security with me as it ushered in his awareness of the world.

Or, it could have just been gas.

Not only am I interpreting his actions, he is also interpreting mine. When he toddles up to my leg and raises his arms, he is communicating that he wants to be picked up. When he points to something, he is saying he wants it or is interested in it. Unless these gestures are mutually understood, confusion reigns. If I didn't pick him up when he raised his arms, and gave him a drink instead, he might associate raising his arms with drink. There is an essential give and take between a baby and his world that fosters his development of language.

As weeks and months go by, he continues assimilating, associating and understanding more and more about his world based on his experiences, his abilities and what he sees.

Then comes speech. Babies move quickly from uttering sounds to using words and sentences. Eventually the young child becomes a proficient communicator and begins to socialize with the rest of the world.

But what happens when the brain doesn't develop correctly and this complex system doesn't function the way it was intended? Language becomes an unwitting victim. In autism, it's as if someone threw a stone into the liquid that is the brain as it is developing. The ripples affect every corner of the autistic person's being.

It was Ned's first day in my classroom, Ned having recently moved from Ohio. Ned was a tiny boy with a pointy noise, brown eyes and a page boy haircut. He was as light as a feather and did not talk, only grunting and moaning in what often sounded like a long hum.

I wanted to make him feel at ease and unafraid on his first day in our program so I called him over, picked him up and put him on my lap during our morning socialization time.

"Hi, Ned, how are you today?" I said, smiling.

Ned took one look at me, drew back his hand and hit me in the face, so hard the force knocked out one of my contacts and deposited it somewhere on the floor of my room.

Then he jumped from my lap and ran back to his seat.

So much for making him feel at ease.

The smack was his way of communicating to me that he wanted to be left alone. However, aggression can be a defining moment. Either he was going to teach me that when he hits I'd better leave him alone, or I was going to teach him that hitting was inappropriate and would not be tolerated. After taking a standing ten count, I put a little ice on my eye and prepared to teach Ned a little about communication.

I walked back to him, this time keeping a more respectable distance.

"Hi, Ned, how are you today?" I repeated the exact sentence that got me clobbered last time.

This time I caught his right hook before it landed.

"NO!" I said, loudly and sternly.

"Hi, Ned." I repeated, holding his hand.

Apparently he was as determined as I was. He tried to hit me with his left hand. I caught it as well.

"NO!" I repeated.

Again I tried to say hi, and he responded with a kick.

"NO!"

I tried another hi and he tried another kick, which I blocked.

"Hi Ned," I repeated.

We were face to face, his offense against my defense, both determined to prevail.

"Uh," he grunted, shaking his head.

That was all I was looking for, a response to my hi, so I accepted it.

"Good job, Ned," I said, smiling. I patted him on the shoulder and sent him back to his seat.

"You won," Dolly said. "You won."

"Yea," I acknowledged, holding the ice pack to my ever-blackening eye. "I'm just glad he wasn't an octopus."

Over time Ned came to enjoy our good morning routine. Although he never spoke in words we could understand, he always gave us his best grunt and he never tried to hit me again.

Not long after that encounter with Ned, Tammy joined my classroom. Tammy was a 16 year-old nonverbal young lady with long strawberry blond hair that sat Raggedy Ann-like on her head. She had brown eyes, stood 5'5" tall and weighed around 125 pounds.

One way of working with nonverbal students is to find something they like and use it to elicit a response. A universal motivation is food (Linda's "mama" burst forth from a package of M&M's). Consequently, lunch is a good time to work on speech. Tammy loved to eat and particularly loved the milk that came with her school lunch. My plan was to let her eat first, then when she was good and thirsty hold her milk ransom until I got some kind of response.

She sat at a corner table in my room and I sat across from her. She ate from her lunch tray while watching me dubiously. When she reached for her milk, I got it first and held it up in view.

"Tammy," I began with a smile, "milk."

"Milk," I repeated, showing her the milk again, continuing to smile.

Tammy looked at the milk, then back at me, then went back to eating.

My mind wandered back to Linda and how, by this time, she would be smiling her sly little smile. I was awakened from my reverie when I felt Tammy's hand on the milk carton I was holding. I sat up and watched her lips, waiting for some sound. I should have watched her hands. In one swift move that would have made Bruce Lee proud, she grabbed the carton out of my hand and smashed it down on my head. As the milk cascaded over my face one of my contacts went with it. Before I had time to catch it, Tammy threw her tray, with the rest of her lunch, into my chest and onto my lap.

I was determined that she not get reinforced from this behavior, so I kept trying. I was going to get language out of her, even if she made me into a smorgasbord.

I grabbed another milk carton from another lunch tray and kept pushing Tammy until she finally uttered something. Then I let her have the milk. Tammy quickly began to understand what I wanted. She'd make a sound when she wanted milk and eventually learned to point to a picture when it was presented to her. She started communicating and I didn't have to endure another milk bath.

I found it symbolic that in the heat of battles with Ned and Tammy I lost two contacts. They were asking me to see them through a different set of eyes. Both times I found the contact when I was cleaning up, just as I heard the crunch of it breaking underfoot. I didn't welcome losing my contacts, smelling like sour milk or having a black eye. But I realized that while bruises heal, and I can buy new contacts or wash milk out of my hair, autism is permanent. There really is no comparison.

Standing close to Linda's mom, so full of joy as she cradled Linda in her arms. Peering at Tammy through a soft ivory coating of milk as she tried to talk. Watching a red-hot Ned slowly cool off as we found a better way to communicate. Looking into the twinkling eyes of Ethan as he happily typed his little messages. Watching the expectations of my students rise, bathed in the silence of understanding. Yes, there are moments in our lives that are forever imprinted on our brains, that fill us with wonder and replenish our soul.

Chapter Thirteen
Labels, Labels, Labels

*M*y eyesight is not perfect. Without glasses, I can't see the biggest letter on the eye chart; in fact, I can't even see the eye chart! It is something I have come to accept over the years. Although annoying at times, it is correctable and has not been a hindrance to the quality of my life. With glasses I have no trouble seeing the diverse, uniquely beautiful details of the world. Without them, my view becomes a Monet of foggy images that run together like the hues on an artist's palette.

At times my eyesight has been a source of laughter. We have home movies of me at a swimming pool, waving to some unknown person while my children struggle to turn me in the direction of the camera. At other times it has been a source of frustration. I was self-conscious about my glasses throughout high school and hated wearing them in public. And, at times it has been a source of pain. Kids called me "four eyes"; it was an unwelcome label.

As a society, we have an unusual need to label people. Perhaps it evolves from a need to know our heritage:

why we are the way we are and why we act the way we act. Whatever the reason, we classify. This person is Italian, that one is Jewish. He's gay, she's old, he's fat, she's pretty. We have labels for everything. Normally this is not a problem, but I believe if we are not careful a person's true identity, his essence, is lost in the myriad of classifications and distinctions we so arbitrarily bestow on them. We use labels to highlight differences, a mistake that can, and does, lead to intolerance, prejudice and discrimination when we react to the label instead of the person.

It is no different with autism. How do parents cope with the ubiquity of the label and its ensuing problems? There is no simple answer. Initially the label gives parents an explanation, a shared understanding, as well as an avenue of hope. But it soon feels like riding a roller coaster in the dark, never knowing when the next crest or canyon will appear. I have seen parents who ride the coaster with their eyes shut, denying there is a problem. I have seen others whose valleys are long and deep. They seem angry and cast blame like beads at a Mardi Gras parade. I have seen parents who seem to have accepted their ride with courage and dignity and live a wonderful life, incorporating autism into it. Mostly, I have seen parents who are holding on for dear life to a ride they did not choose, careening over hills and valleys not of their own making, while trying to retain their integrity, sanity and some semblance of quality of life.

Some labels, like autism, are hard to accept. I'm not sure we ever accept them. My wife's mother passed on years ago. She has accepted this. Yet not a day goes by that she doesn't wish it hadn't happened and her mom would walk through the door and back into our lives. So, it is I think, with autism.

As a teacher, my reaction to the label of autism is different than for a parent. I see it solely as a means of placing students into my class; nothing else. I know the person who enters my group will be a unique and varied individual, unlike any other in my room.

Reggie certainly fit the label of autism, right down to its clinical definition. He talked in long deep monotones like Lurch on the "Addams Family," but not spontaneously or socially. He was 18 when I met him, a tall young man with coal black hair that sat in a permanent wave on his thin, oblong head. He had dark brown eyes set deeply into his face, accentuating his zombie-like appearance.

Reggie was an Idiot Savant, a badly worded label. In the 1970's and 1980's, it was used to represent the three percent of the population in the U.S. who were retarded, and/or autistic, yet possessed extraordinary talent in one or more areas. Fortunately, the label has altruistically been replaced in recent years with the less insulting term, Savant Syndrome. Paul's odd knowledge of shoes and Russell's extensive familiarity with classical music would fall into this category. Reggie was a whiz with numbers. If you gave him a date, he could instantly tell you on what day of the week it occurred. He never missed. In most other areas, however—reading, reading comprehension, and thinking—he was very limited.

Reggie was an endearing young man, usually very gentle and compliant. When frustrated however, he would cry and moan at the top of his lungs, immediately followed by biting his palm, much like we would bite into an apple. Fortunately, he was not frustrated often. Unfortunately, when he was, I was usually the reason.

Reggie became frustrated when I refused to let him drink, a fact that annoyed him terribly. I only wish water or milk was the culprit, but it wasn't that easy. If we didn't watch Reggie, he would drink the most astonishing and disgusting things. He drank glue, rubber cement, and paint, among other things. In fact, if it poured, he would drink it. As Reggie was one in a class of many students, we couldn't constantly watch his every move, nor could we lock up every liquid in his life. It quickly became apparent that we had to teach him what he could and could not drink.

Over the years I've heard many criticisms about handling particularly difficult behaviors:

"If you knew he was going to drink it, why didn't you stop him?"

"You knew he was a biter, why weren't you more careful?"

"Why weren't you watching?"

The fact is, we did know, we did watch and we were careful. The challenge comes in understanding the difference in the minds of the two parties concerned. My mind, and those of the people who live and work in this field, are filled with many thoughts throughout the day. Many people with autism have one-track minds. In Reggie's case, it was the alcoholic-like urge to drink anything in liquid form. I had to watch a classroom of students; Reggie perseverated on drinking. My only hope was to catch him in the act and teach him not to do it. Hence, the source of our mutual frustration.

I remember the first time I experienced Reggie's unusual thirst. I had been alerted to his drinking problem from the first day, but had seen nothing to indicate there was a problem. So, after a few weeks, I relaxed. We were eating lunch in our room, which we often do, when I looked up from my desk to survey my class.

"Reggie," I said, noticing his milk mustache, "wipe your mouth, please."

He complied.

"Jim," Dollie stammered.

"Yes," I replied, not looking up.

"Jim, Reggie doesn't drink milk. Remember, he's allergic to it."

I had forgotten this tidbit of information. I looked at Reggie hoping that he picked up an errant carton of lactose; he hadn't.

I arrived at his desk just as he polished off the remainder of our white Tempra paint. It often amazed me that a boy could be allergic to milk, yet not to these other things he so willingly ingested. Luckily, Reggie made it through my program without drinking himself to death.

He was my first student to age out of school. The public school system has an obligation to educate students until they are 21 years old, recently changed to 22. After that, the responsibility shifts to an adult agency. Back then, communication between the two groups was contemptible. Many students would leave school to sit at home or worse, end up in institutions. When Reggie turned 21, his mother made it quite clear that she didn't want him living with her any more. His father was nowhere to be found. We were his only hope, so we took to the streets, looking for an appropriate placement for him. Finding a place for older individuals with autism, especially those who still exhibited somewhat bizarre behaviors, was not easy at that time. In Reggie's case, it was next to impossible.

Ironically, it was his label of autism that became his worst obstacle. It hung around his neck like an albatross.

Nancy and I visited many adult agencies. Time and time again we were told the same thing.

"If his label was mental retardation, we could help him. His file says he is autistic."

At first we were dumbfounded. Reggie certainly was mentally retarded; he fit that criterion. But we were given no more than cold stares and negative responses.

Finally, after attempting the truth until we were blue in the face, we did the next best thing. We altered his paperwork. Overnight we changed his label from autistic to mentally retarded.

At the next agency we were met with open arms. Reggie moved into an adult group home and we went about our business.

A year later I heard that Reggie was doing fine. I have since lost contact with him, but I imagine there have been many unexplained disappearances of liquids in that group home over the years.

Reggie's dilemma also brought into focus how polarizing a label can be. As a person with autism, he was unacceptable for a group home. As a person with mental retardation, he was welcomed. Either way, it was still Reggie. His label, like most, became an injustice. It gave people permission, even justification, to define him by his differences, rather than embrace his similarities.

Often I think that people who try to separate us into exclusive and prohibitive categories have lost site of the big picture of life and are seeing the world too much in black and white. Each time this happens, the Reggies of the world suffer, and the rest of us lose a little of our clarity.

I think we all would do better to see the world through less than perfect eyes. Then every discriminating separation would become vague, every apparent distinction cloudy, and every visible difference, hazy. Perhaps then the world would overlook its labels and disparities and become united and whole and beautiful.

Come to think of it, perhaps my eyesight isn't that bad after all.

Chapter Fourteen

Aggression—No Easy Answers

*L*iving in Florida, a person becomes acutely aware of the weather. Hurricanes that form off the coast of Africa can arrive with little warning. Tornadoes come swirling down from a thundercloud with lightning that illuminates the night sky like fireworks. We often don't know how hard they will hit or how much damage will be done.

Fate is like the weather of our souls. It, too, can hit without warning, disrupting our lives and leaving in its path destruction and despair. It's often how we weather these external and internal storms that determines who we are and what our lives become.

Autism has its own weather patterns and one of its "storms" is aggression. A small portion of people with autism exhibit aggression, either to themselves or others. The effects of aggression are devastating, exasperating and long lasting. It exists differently in each person. If you ask ten people about it, you may get ten different answers. Because there are no easy answers in dealing with aggressive behaviors, it often becomes the ultimate test of our ability to handle adversity. While I'd like to believe that we all handle it with integrity, strength and grace, I know that isn't the case, especially when dealing with individuals with autism.

Since treating aggression is such a controversial issue, many school systems, faced with the threat of potential lawsuits, take a strict two-pronged approach: first, teach them and second, do not touch them.

When I was a teenager, I was passing a swimming hole that had a NO SWIMMING sign posted. As I neared the water I heard a person screaming for help. I chose to ignore the posted rule and swam in to save this young boy. Was I right or wrong in ignoring the posted sign? This same dilemma faces teachers of aggressive students today. We are told to help the students who are pulling themselves and others under with their aggressive behaviors, but not to get wet in the process.

I am a firm believer that behavior is communication, especially for many nonverbal or limited verbal children with autism. I also believe that to stop their assaults, we must create a safe environment for them, using positive reinforcement, changes in their surroundings and program structure. The only way we can help them is to dive in, fight the aggression when and where it occurs and teach them that it is not acceptable. This often means grabbing their hands and saying 'NO' or holding them down when they attack.

Perhaps sometimes we have to ignore the NO SWIMMING sign, jump into the water and take our chances. We just may pull someone out.

Danny came to my classroom with a reputation. He had been at Nina Harris when he was younger and had since been moved all over the county because of his violent behaviors. His parents also came with a reputation. They were angry, well read on autism, influential and politically savvy. They insisted that Danny was not violent, and that many of his problems stemmed from the poor education he had received to this point. Therefore our principal, Mr. Green, agreed that I would not be told of Danny's aggression beforehand. Instead, I was told just the opposite. Since Danny's reputation was widespread among the faculty, I found his decision rather odd. Why would he go out of his way to tell me a student wasn't violent, especially when it was common knowledge that he was? Did he think I hadn't heard or was he just trying to appease the parents?

"Don't worry," Mr. Green said. "Danny is not violent. Everything will be OK."

Sure. I was getting a student whom everyone knew was aggressive. I would be watched closely by his parents, the administration and as near as I could tell, the rest of western civilization. Nothing to worry about?

When he first arrived at Nina, Danny was a tall young man with wavy red hair and a face-full of freckles. Although he was non-verbal, a constant stream of sounds emanated from his lips. He liked to keep objects in his hands, constantly moving them back and forth like a juggler. Danny was also very strong physically, and in spite of his parents and Mr. Green's assertions to the contrary, he was violent, extremely violent. He would hit, scratch or bite when he didn't want to comply, which was just about all the time. He was also a head-butter. When you got too close behind him, he would jerk back his head, hitting your face or whatever body part was nearby. Rumor was at his last school, he put two teachers in the hospital with his head. Because of his violence, I decided that initially, I would be the only person working with Danny.

Our first day together arrived. I asked Danny to come to another part of the classroom with me; he didn't move. I walked up beside him and repeated my request. Again, he didn't budge. As I started to put my hand on his shoulder, he jerked his head back hard and fast. Although I was expecting this, I was not about to stop and reason with Danny about why his head-butt was not an acceptable behavior. So, once I grabbed his neck, I pushed his head back down to the table.

"NO!" I said, as loudly as I could.

Fortunately the neck muscles pushing back are not too strong. I was able to keep his head down while I repeatedly said 'no' into his ear, hoping he got the message.

Danny needed to know that his head butting was not going to work and that when he tried it, he was going to be uncomfortable. He had to have a reason for wanting to stop butting. The procedure proved effective.

In the midst of working with Danny, we were told we were getting another new student.

"Big John is his name," Mr. Green said, at a meeting of what were now four teachers in autism. "From what we hear, he is extremely violent. We've decided since Jim has Danny, that we will put John into Cindy's classroom."

"So let me get this straight, " I said. "You are not putting John in my class because he is violent, because you don't want him around Danny, who is not?"

I probably should have kept my mouth shut, but the irony was too good to pass up. It didn't matter as he chose to ignore me, and Big John was placed into Cindy's classroom. Only a large corrugated curtain, which we kept partially opened, separated my room from Cindy's. I would be close by if she needed help.

It was also decided that Bob, our school's behavior specialist, and Mr. Green would sit in the room the first day as well.

Big John lived up to his reputation. He was big, mean and intimidating. He stood 6'3" tall and weighed close to 230 pounds. Cindy was a petite 5'2". I was glad Bob and Mr. Green were going to be in her room.

Soon after John arrived I heard a loud SMACK come from Cindy's room, then another SMACK, and another. When I heard the fourth smack I decided to investigate.

Cindy was trying to run a group activity at the table. Every time she approached Big John he would smack her with his flat hand.

"Good morning, John."

SMACK on her back.

"How are you, John?"

SMACK on her arm.

Cindy looked quizzically at the two 'helpers' sitting in the back of her room. They didn't budge.

I watched the behavior specialist busily writing on a clipboard and the principal calmly watching the proceedings.

I became furious and the next time Big John hit Cindy I ran to him, grabbed him by the back of his neck and put him on the floor.

"NO." I said loudly. "NO HITTING."

"Bob, what in the world were you doing?" I asked our behavior specialist.

"I was taking baseline data," he replied.

Now, I understand the importance of collecting data to chart whether or not improvement has occurred as a result of treatment. You may recall that Linda's hand biting increased using Anbesol, showing me that my intervention was not only failing, but working in the opposite direction. However, I am not so sure the concept applies in the same way when a person is physically assaulting another person. I believe aggression needs to be stopped immediately.

"A baseline!" I shouted, looking back at Cindy. "Next time take the baseline while he's hitting you."

I felt John needed to know from the first attack that his aggression would not be tolerated. By letting it go on, even for a short time, we were reinforcing his behavior, making any subsequent procedure we tried difficult to implement. I felt it far more important to show John his aggression would not be tolerated first, than to take baseline data.

It still amazes me how two professionals could sit and watch a student continually hit another human being. I understand my students have unique problems, brought on by equally unique situations. I know it's our responsibility to work through behaviors that are sometimes bizarre. However, this does not mean that we needlessly take abuse in the name of data collection.

Big John's aggression ebbed, even without that baseline. Unfortunately, he was only with us for a short time before he moved away again. I only hope his next teacher is spared the good intentions of a well meaning, if not slightly bungling, behavior therapists.

One of the drawbacks of my using aggression to deal with aggression is that it only taught the student that he should not become violent while I was in the room. But, I believe it is a start that, when coupled with other techniques, gives us a foothold. Sometimes, however, that foothold is shaky.

Danny knew I was the only person strong enough to control him. Therefore, I became the only teacher who could work with him without him becoming aggressive. This meant I was always on alert when someone else was around Danny; I couldn't take anything for granted.

One day my assistant, Deborah, was bringing Danny into the classroom from the bus, as she did every morning. This was an unobtrusive task and Danny always complied without a problem. I was in the room preparing for the day when I heard a faint cry for help.

"Jim!" came the distant frightened scream.

Instantly I knew it was Deborah and that she was in trouble. I ran down the hall to find Deborah, who was pregnant at the time, on the floor with Danny on top of her.

"Danny," I cried, grabbing his neck and pulling him off Deborah.

"NO," I said, pinning him to the ground.

He knew when I arrived it was time to give up, and he did.

Another time Deborah informed Danny that it was time for lunch. Again, another mundane task she had done many times without incident. Danny would go to the sink, wash his hands and prepare for lunch. On this day when Deborah neared him, he bit her hand.

Deborah went to the hospital for a shot and I filled out the accident report. Under 'Cause' I wrote: *Danny bit her.* Short, sweet and to the point. At the end of the day Mr. Green called me into his office. He stood there, glaring at me, waving my accident report in his hand.

"What are you trying to do?" he said, shaking the report in my face.

"What are you talking about?" I asked.

"This accident report," he said, still shaking it. "You said Danny bit Deborah."

"Yes, sir," I said, still somewhat befuddled. "That's what happened."

"You can't put that in the report," he said. "Do you know what his mother will do?"

"Mr. Green, the truth is that Danny bit Deborah. What do you want me to say?"

"You don't have to say that it was Danny," he said.

"Who would you prefer?" I asked, wondering why he was so angry with me. After all, I didn't bite Deborah.

"I want you to redo this report and write that Deborah was bitten by a student, no names, understand?" he said, tossing the report into my lap.

"Mr. Green, we need to tell the truth. His mother can't dictate what we write in an accident report."

"Just redo the report Jim," he said, ignoring me. "And get it back to me by tomorrow."

I consider myself easy to get along with, but I strongly felt that he was wrong. If he wasn't going to take a stand, I was.

"Mr. Green," I said, laying the report on his desk. "This report is already done and it is accurate."

I turned and left the room.

I later learned that Mr. Green redid the report to his liking.

I still believe I was right. However, what started out as a matter of principle just became a matter of principal.

Perhaps there are some students we are just not equipped to deal with in a public school setting. They need more help than we can possibly offer. Marty was one; most likely Linda was too. Certainly Danny was such a student. As my class size grew, it became extremely difficult to run an entire classroom while protecting myself and every other person from Danny, while receiving no support from the principal.

There came a time when I needed to convey this sentiment. However, amidst the climate of fear and intimidation that was prevalent, the message became misconstrued.

"If you don't want Danny in your class, then we'll move him to another school," his mom insisted.

Strange as it may sound I liked Danny. Yes, he was challenging, but there was something endearing about him. However, I knew he was getting bigger and was already becoming stronger than me. He needed a program designed for severe aggression and constant care. If he didn't get it, he was going to hurt someone someday—severely.

Although everyone heard my pleas, they ignored them. As far as they were concerned, if I was unable to handle Danny, they would simply find someone else who could.

Eventually he was moved to another school with a principal who told Danny's mother what she wanted to hear—that her son wasn't aggressive. Perhaps my problem was solved, but not Danny's. Despite the new principal's assertions on how good Danny was doing, he still managed to put two people in the hospital.

In retrospect, I still feel we were ill-equipped to handle Danny's particular type of violence. I understood the school system's reluctance in admitting we were unable to handle him. It would mean finding and funding a private program. But I have never understood why his mom was hesitant. She knew her rights and she knew a private program was an option. If she had pushed for it, she would have received it. Why keep him in a place she continually said couldn't do the job? Wasn't she teaching us a lesson at his expense?

It remains a mystery to me.

I believe we failed Danny, just as we fail every student with aggressive behaviors if we don't face them, jump in and deal with them.

When the winds of adversity blow, there's a possibility we may get swept away. If we are lucky enough to bend like a tree under the strain, when the storm is over, we may have learned a little about honesty, integrity, tolerance and encouragement. When the sky returns to blue, we are hopeful that we know a little more about ourselves and move forward better prepared for the next storm, already brewing on the horizon.

Chapter Fifteen

The Key that Unlocks the Door

*T*he famed psychologist, Abraham Maslow, developed a theory purporting that humans are what he termed, "wanting animals." Humans, Maslow theorized, possess a hierarchy of needs. Those needs on the bottom of the heirarchy must be satisfied before a person can address needs that exist at the higher levels. Maslow's bottom level was basic physiological needs, food and water, for instance. The need for safety and shelter comes next. It makes sense. Only after our needs for food and shelter are met does a person even think about love. The progression of needs continues until a person becomes, in Maslow's words, "self-actualized."

Maslow's theory applies to education, too. If a student does not have food or shelter, s/he cannot begin to worry about learning. On the scale of what's important, learning will always fall behind surviving. Once basic needs are fulfilled however, learning can take place.

When Darlene arrived at our program, she was definitely at the bottom level of Maslow's hierarchy. She came from a county to the north of ours, at a time when they had no place for her.

"I hate to say this, but she's like a little animal," her school's administrator said to me after observing my classroom. "We need to get her into school, but she's so uncontrollable."

"Despite that," she said, realizing she wasn't doing such a good selling job, "I think you'll like her and I'm sure she'll do fine here."

"Like a little animal? What do you mean?" I asked, intrigued by her description.

"Well, she doesn't speak, doesn't like to stay dressed, seldom keeps her shoes on her feet and destroys every class she enters. We've tried her in three different classrooms now with no success."

"Sounds exciting," I said, as visions of Linda ran through my head. "Does she wear glasses?"

"No, she's never been tested. She won't sit long enough."

The necessary arrangements were made. A bus from Darlene's county would be transporting her from home to our program, a trip of about an hour and a half each way. Darlene would have her own driver and her own assistant every day for the three-hour round trip. Although it was a long and expensive excursion, the school system was willing to provide the service. Either they were very impressed with my class or they really wanted to get rid of her!

"Here we go," I said, as Darlene's bus arrived for her first day at Nina. Before we could welcome her, Darlene had burst off the bus in her bare feet, passed Deborah and me, whom she had never met, and continued into the building.

"Where is she going?" Deborah asked, looking at me.

"I don't know," I shrugged. "But she seems in an awful hurry to get there."

I walked to the bus and introduced myself while Deborah hunted down Darlene.

"Hi, I'm Jim," I said. The driver and assistant were too frazzled to speak.

"Did you have a nice trip?"

Al, the driver, was the first to speak.

"Wow, they told me she'd be a handful," he said, shaking his head. "But we couldn't get her to stay in her seat. She was running all over the bus."

"Oh my," was all the assistant, Jane, could muster before falling back into her seat on the bus.

"Thanks! We'll take it from here. Go get some rest. After all, you have to take her home. Are these hers?" I asked picking up a pair of old sneakers and socks from the front of the bus.

Jane nodded and waved her hand.

"She wouldn't keep them on."

"Is here anything else I should know?"

Al and Jane looked at each other.

"Good luck," they said simultaneously as the bus pulled away. "See you at 3:30."

As I returned to the classroom Deborah was entering with Darlene in tow.

"I found her in the cafeteria," she said. "She was stealing donuts."

"Hi Darlene," I said, as Deborah literally handed her off to me.

At this point we were fearful of letting her go.

She nodded and smiled. Her smile was a carbon copy of Linda's, with that same sparkle in her eye.

"This is going to be fun," I thought to myself.

My first job was to get her into a seat and keep her there. Sitting is a basic building block to teaching. If I couldn't get her to sit, how could I ever expect her to do anything?

I put her in a chair and she got up and ran. I caught her, put her in the seat and up she went again. This went on for a while. Desperate, I looked around for something that might hold her attention. I tried puzzles, blocks, books, anything I could reach, to no avail.

One of the challenges of my job is to discover what things will motivate my students to pay attention and learn. As food is one of our most basic needs, it's often a great place to start with a student like Darlene.

Remembering Darlene's initial foray into the cafeteria, I asked Deborah to return there and bring back something sweet. Forget good nutrition; it was time to bring in the big guns—donuts! I was counting on Darlene's sweet tooth to help us both succeed.

The next time Darlene jumped up from her seat, I was ready. I raised my donut out of its hiding place, like a cowboy unholsters his gun.

Darlene eyed it with some interest.

"You want this?" I asked, showing her the donut. "If you want it, come here and sit," I said, patting her seat.

Darlene cocked her head from one side to the other.

I put the donut on her desk.

She looked at me, hesitated, walked over to her seat, picked up the donut and was about to take a bite.

Quickly I snatched it from her grasp.

"No, Darlene," I said. "If you want it you need to sit down."

Again I patted the chair.

I sat down in the chair next to her desk.

"See," I said, taking a bite of the donut. "Um, this is good."

(I have always been willing to sacrifice my diet for one of my students. It's a gift).

Darlene again hesitated, then sat down in the chair. I handed her the donut. In the middle of devouring it, she looked at me and smiled.

We were rolling. She made the basic connection that I wanted her in her seat and would pay handsomely for it.

Next we worked on her shoes. We were able to use food as a reinforcer here, as well. We progressed from sitting for a donut to sitting with her shoes and socks on for a donut. Darlene learned quickly and in a few short weeks, she would come into the room with her shoes on (they were using donuts on the bus as well) and sit down in her seat.

Over a period of weeks, we slowly progressed to having Darlene join us for activities. When she would falter and jump out of her seat I never chased her. Instead I would give everyone who was sitting as they should a donut.

"OK," I'd say when Darlene was out of her seat. "Everyone sitting, let's have a donut." Darlene would run to her seat but it was too late; I would have already eaten hers.

Periodically throughout the day when Darlene was staying seated, she would also join us in having a donut. We did this so that she never knew when reinforcement was coming, but firmly understood that it would only come when she was in her seat.

It worked! After only a few months of bartering, Darlene would come into school with her shoes and socks on her feet, go to her seat and didn't have to be rewarded daily with a donut.

At approximately the same time Darlene joined the program, Tammy started exhibiting a new behavior that had us both baffled and concerned. At the end of the day when we'd mention it was time to get ready for the bus to go home, she would have a bowel movement in her pants. Since we would have to clean her up before sending her home, she was late and the bus would be late. To make matters worse, we were sending her home every day with a bag of dirty pants, which didn't make her parents very happy.

Try as we might, we couldn't come up with a reason for her behavior. We checked to see if there was a problem on the bus; there wasn't. We wondered if there was a new problem at home. Nope. As we continued to look for an explanation, a theory started to surface: what if there wasn't a major problem in her life? What if her behavior was only an indication that she needed to use the bathroom each day before getting on the bus? Tammy didn't speak, so perhaps she was communicating in the only way she knew how. It was worth checking out.

The next day when it was time to get ready for the bus, I asked Tammy to go to the bathroom. She complied. When I thought she had had sufficient time to settle on the toilet, I made my announcement.

"Tammy, its time to get ready for the bus," I said outside the bathroom door.

I heard a loud grunt from inside the bathroom. In a few minutes Tammy came out. Her pants were clean and dry and she had relieved herself in the toilet. She washed her hands, grabbed her backpack and went out the door.

The next day, buoyed by our initial success, we tried again. Sure enough, the same thing happened.

The following day when I asked her to use the bathroom, I placed a picture of the bathroom in front of her.
I asked her to hand it to me, waited until she was settled,
made my announcement and voila! Within a week she
was handing us the picture whenever she wanted to use
the restroom.

What happened? Before then, Tammy had had no
problem with toileting. Why the behavior change all of
a sudden? I realized that we were being too careful in
meeting her needs. Tammy had never had an accident
because we made sure she used the restroom regularly.
She never had to communicate with us because we never
gave her the chance. We would make sure she used the
restroom in the afternoon and that was that. Perhaps her
metabolism changed and she needed to use the restroom
before going home. But we hadn't given her a way to
communicate that to us, so she just let it out the only way
she knew how. When given a more appropriate way to
communicate, she was more than happy to use it.

Since Darlene lived an hour and a half away, her
mother never made a visit to Nina. We used a daily notebook that went back and forth and a weekly telephone
call to communicate. My first conversation with her was
revealing. She was at her wit's end, unable to handle Darlene in any way. Her only recourse was to put her out in
the back yard, which was fenced and locked, because she
was too disruptive inside the house. Darlene would eat at
the picnic bench in the covered porch that sheltered her
from the rain. When it was time for bed they would pick
her up, undress her, and put her in the shower. When
she was clean they would dress her and put her into bed.

Her windows were boarded up and the door locked from the outside. In the morning they would get her up, dress her, then take her to the back porch for breakfast. When the bus arrived they would pick her up, carry her to it, give her a kiss, hand her shoes and socks to the assistant, then put Darlene on the bus.

This was their life. No one visited them, having long ago been frightened away. Darlene's parents hid her in the back yard not because they were cruel but because it was the only way they knew to cope with the situation. Their family was in a state of disarray, with Darlene smack dab in the center. They truly loved her but didn't know what to do for her.

Once we learned the secret power of donuts, we passed this information on to Darlene's parents. They too began to experience success. We were lucky that Darlene loved food and were able to improve her behaviors, and her quality of life, by using it. After a short period of time Darlene was living inside the house, eating at the table and even watching TV with her family. Isn't it amazing how a daily routine, something we take for granted, can be the source of enormous happiness to others?

Sometimes all the formal education in the world takes a back seat to tried and true observation, perseverance and a little good luck. Teaching can be an unpredictable profession, especially in the area of special education. Sometimes you have to throw away the books and forget what you've been taught in college. With close observation and a keen eye, it's possible to see what our students are trying to tell us and learn what they need from us. If you are lucky, you may even begin to understand them.

At the end of the school year we heard that Darlene would not be coming back to Nina. Apparently her school district no longer wanted to spend the money to have her attend our program, and decided to start a class of their own. Tammy was moved to another program and I never saw nor heard from her again.

I believe we helped Darlene and Tammy take the difficult first steps up Maslow's stairway. As they began their journey through the hierarchy, it became clear to me that as we help our students advance to new levels of development, we can't help but move up ourselves.

Chapter Sixteen
Traditions

*I*t was a great time to be at Nina. Darlene was staying seated most of the time and Tammy was accident free. We were ready to celebrate.

Partying has been a custom in my class. We celebrate holidays, birthdays, anniversaries, changes in the weather, Fridays—you name it, we've celebrated it. Birthdays were an especially favorite occasion and, as luck would have it, Jack was having a birthday. Our tradition is to send the birthday boy or girl out of the room. Then we light the candles on the birthday cake and turn off all the lights. He returns to everyone singing Happy Birthday, as he blows out the candles. Every student I have ever taught has loved this moment. Everyone except Jack.

Jack was a short young man with light brown hair parted on the side. He had a long face, brown eyes and the wisps of a mustache on his upper lip, which was in constant motion, as Jack talked to himself continuously. Even though he had limited verbal ability and didn't make much sense, he loved conversing with people. (I know a few non-autistic people with this same attribute.) He reminded me of a little old man who, partially senile, talks to himself or anyone around and goes on talking even after that person has departed.

Jack especially loved sports. I don't believe he understood what was going on in the game, but he loved the action and, in particular, the referees. He loved to imitate them. Jack would pretend to blow a whistle then move his arms to signal off-sides, traveling, or strike three. It didn't matter if his sports were mixed up; he loved what the men in stripes did.

When I was reprimanding someone Jack might pretend to blow his whistle and signal offside. If someone was running in the hallway he would stand in the way, blow his fake whistle and signal stop. If I moved to a particular section of the room, he would blow the whistle and signal touchdown. Although we never knew exactly when his umpire mode would appear, his calls were always right on target and he never disappointed us.

I was unaware that Jack hated birthday parties until the first time we attempted to celebrate his. He seemed a little uneasy as we asked him to leave the room.

"Tweet" he blew his fake whistle. "Time out" he said, waving his hands over his head. "Time out" he repeated as he left.

We prepared the room and the candles for Jack's return.

"OK Jack, we're ready," I said, as I opened the door. "Come on back in."

Jack was shaking his head and calling time out over and over again.

"Jack," I repeated. "Don't you want to blow out your candles?"

"Tweet. Mr. Yerman, come here." He motioned me over after calling time out. "I don't want to go in there. No birthday party. No birthday party. No way. No way."

Since the candles were burning down all over the cake, I had to choose between making him go through what was my perception of a happy party or respecting his individuality.

"Jack," I said, patting him on the shoulder. "Wait here. I'll be right back."

Entering the room, I explained to everyone that we would sing Happy Birthday to Jack while he was in the hallway, then blow out his candles and cut his cake before he came back into the room.

We sang to an empty chair, blew out the candles together, cut the cake, then invited Jack in to eat it with us.

This became our tradition of celebrating Jack's birthday.

I believe in traditions and think it's important to grow up with them. They're like an invisible glue that repeatedly cements a group together. At times, out of necessity, traditions can and should be modified or updated.

After my divorce and remarriage, the traditional Christmas morning of a family opening their presents was impossible to follow. There were too many parents and houses. My wife and children came up with a new tradition. On Christmas Eve we would order pizza and open presents. We'd then take a ride, looking at Christmas lights as we sang carols playing on the radio. Then we'd drop the kids at their other parents' houses for Christmas morning. This became our tradition; we all loved it and looked forward to it each year.

Jack's unique way of celebrating became a tradition we looked forward to as well. Everyone, including the birthday boy, was happy. When I shared it with Jack's mother, she was ecstatic. She had long ago canceled celebrating his birthday since it was so upsetting for him. Now she began upholding his new tradition at home as well.

GUS was referred to my class by way of an emotionally handicapped classroom in another school in the county. At the time he started with us, he was running away daily.

Gus stood 5'2" tall, had blond hair and a round face with soft features. He was an extremely innocent, passive and sweet person. It was this innocence, I believe, that prompted him to run away. The other students, on a daily basis, were unmercifully tormenting Gus. His only recourse was to flee.

This proved to be the case, as he never ran from my classroom. His "problem" behavior corrected itself without intervention. A change in environment, albeit to one of emotional safety and security, was all he needed. I've learned over the years that sometimes it's the program that's the problem, not the student.

Gus had some unique abilities and interests. He knew all about game shows. He loved to watch them and knew the name of every show, the host, what time it aired and on what station. He also had a memory for buses. He remembered every bus he ever took in school, as well as the driver's name. To this day Gus calls me at the beginning of each school year to find out what buses are transporting my students. His memory didn't stop there. While he was in our program, Gus acted as our personnel directory. Once told, he remembered every name and phone number and could recall them in an instant. In the dichotomy that is autism though, Gus didn't understand much language and it was difficult to hold a conversation with him.

Gus had one behavior that troubled all of us—he hated red trucks. While we were all outside one day, he began crying. I walked over to him.

"Gus, are you all right?"

"I'm crying," he said.

"I know, Gus. Why are you crying?"

"Red truck" he said, pointing to the road.

"A red truck? You saw a red truck?"

By now the truck had passed.

"What did the red truck do?"

"Red truck," he said, pointing to the road again.

"Gus," I said, placing my hand on his shoulder. "Why are you crying?"

Gus felt his cheeks.

"Because I'm sad," he responded.

"Good. Now Gus, why are you sad?"

"Because I'm crying."

"But why are you crying?"

"Because I'm sad."

This was the vicious circle of Gus' thinking. For two years, whenever he saw a red truck our conversation never wavered. He was unable to give me a clue about his behavior and I was unable to figure it out.

The source of Jack's and Gus' seemingly unusual fears remained a mystery to me. When faced with moments like these in my students' lives, I think about my own children. What would I want for them? In their moments of distress, I would want someone to come over, lay a hand on their shoulder and tell them that everything will be all right.

Until I know better, that's the tradition I'm going to follow.

Chapter Seventeen
There are NO Guarantees

*I*t was mid-November and the four classes in our program were preparing for our annual Thanksgiving dinner. It was a grand affair. Each class was responsible for a portion of the banquet and we took the three days before vacation to create it. We'd open up the partitions that separated our classes and push all the tables together to form one continuous dining table on which we'd spread our feast.

This was Darlene's first Thanksgiving with us. She was doing great at sitting now, but her grooming skills were another matter. Her medium length hair sat in a tousled mess on her head and needed more than brushing. As one of our assistants was a hairdresser, I wrote a note to Darlene's mom asking if we could cut her hair for free. She agreed. The next day Anita gave her the works: a shampoo, cut and blow dry. Darlene loved the attention and what was happening to her. She sat, smiled and laughed. When Anita was finished, everyone thought she looked really cute. Darlene even seemed pleased.

The next day when Darlene exited the bus she ran past us and into the school, just as she had done the first day. I noticed her hair as she passed us.

"What happened, Jane?" I asked, as I picked up her backpack.

"Read the note," she said sadly. "It's a shame, just a shame."

"I'm sorry, Jim," Al declared. "We thought she looked great."

We learned that Darlene's mother was furious. She was so upset with Darlene's haircut that she decided to fix it herself. Unfortunately for Darlene, that consisted of cutting it off completely.

We found her sitting at her seat with her head down.

"Hey Darlene, let's see your new hairdo," I said enthusiastically. I didn't want her to feel any worse than she did already. "Hey Deborah, isn't she beautiful?"

"She sure is."

"Deborah, why don't you take her around and show her new hair-do to everyone else."

As Deborah led Darlene away I wondered what had gone wrong. Perhaps I moved too fast. As Darlene became more comfortable with us and began to improve, I hadn't thought about how these changes were affecting her family, especially her mother. Perhaps we had encroached too much into her territory.

Deborah returned with Darlene, who immediately ran to her seat, smiling. Our attempt at damage control was successful. Darlene recovered from it quickly; her mother never did.

AT that time I had two students in my class with the exact same name: Lenny Smith. They were alike in only a few ways. For the most part, they were as different as night and day.

One Lenny was nonverbal. When asked a question his response was always the same. It didn't matter what he was asked. He would grunt, shake his head, and smile but what an endearing smile.

The other Lenny was verbal. He understood much of what was going on around him, and he had quite a large vocabulary. He was also very social. However, Lenny2 happened to be born with a paralyzed palate, which meant his words came out in a distinctive nasal tone—so nasal that he was difficult to understand. Those of us who had been around him a while could converse with him, but strangers had a hard time understanding him.

As his speech became clearer to me I realized that Lenny2 had one very offensive habit, masked by his impediment. He would swear under his breath.

"Lenny, it's time to get to work," I'd say. "Get your notebook and come here."

"Yes, Mr. Yerman," Lenny would say. "Oh shit," he'd add, in his nasal mumble.

I view Lenny2's behavior as pay back for one of my high school indiscretions involving our gym teacher, Dan Emmit. Mr. Emmit was a yeller. He'd yell our names during roll call, he'd yell if we did something right, and he'd yell if we did something wrong. Underneath his gruff exterior he treated us fairly and even enjoyed a good joke. He would laugh with us one moment and think nothing of swatting us with Big Bertha, his personal paddle, the next.

On the day we discovered his first name, we devised a plan only high school teenagers could enjoy. The next class period during roll call we put our scheme into action.

"Anderson," Mr. Emmit boomed.

"Here, Dan Emmit," my friend Pat Anderson boomed right back. However, he said the two words together so fast it sounded like "Dammit."

Those of us who knew what he was doing laughed at our ingenuity. I remember waiting for my turn, anticipating how wonderful it was going to feel to swear right in front of the teacher. One by one my friends did the "Dan Emmit" rant; each time we'd laugh more and more. I had the unfortunate distinction of being last in the alphabet. By the time Mr. Emmit got to me, he was no longer amused. I was so looking forward to my chance that I failed see his mounting anger.

"Yerman," he boomed.

I decided to add a little pizzazz to my declaration.

"God Dan Emmit," I said. "I'm coming. Keep your pants on."

I busted out laughing and looked over at my friends; they were not laughing along with me.

It was the straw that broke the gym teacher's back. He took out Big Bertha and gave me five hard swats on the spot.

After that we used "Dan Emmit" sparingly in front of him. Many was the time, however, a class would break into laughter, as someone, chastised by a teacher, would mumble "Dan Emmit" under his breath. I had enjoyed our little prank as much as the next person and never thought it would come back to haunt me, until Lenny2 arrived.

"Lenny, would you please open that notebook" I'd say.

"Yes, Mr. Yerman," he'd repeat politely, then throw in under his breath, "dammit."

When I confronted him he would apologize, but I swear I'd hear him mumble something else under his breath as I walked away. I didn't think it necessary to worry excessively about this behavior. Not many people understood him and he really wasn't hurting anyone. My rear end wished Mr. Emmit would have had the same foresight.

Nonverbal Lenny enjoyed food and music while Lenny2 had many areas of interest: black cats, tornadoes, boats, and music, to name a few. He particularly liked black cats and other Halloween decorations.

Music, however, was their common denominator. One Lenny loved to dance and the other loved to listen, which was perfect because one Lenny had rhythm and the other did not. When we played music, Lenny2 would close his eyes to listen, much the same way Ronald did, while the other Lenny would jump out of his seat to dance. He would put one foot in front of the other and bob up and down so enthusiastically that his head would almost touch the floor. Up and down he'd bob until the music ended and he returned to his seat.

We upheld a Thanksgiving tradition where every year, for fun, each class would bake a pumpkin pie to be judged by our supervisor, Mr. Minter. The winner received the coveted golden turkey, an old ceramic fowl of unknown origin.

You never really know a person until you're in a pie-making contest against them. Let me tell you, it is not a pretty sight. Out of the four pies, only one could be the best. This was the third year of the competition and my class had yet to win. Not only did I always lose (two years and two fourth place finishes), but I was sure Cindy had won last year with a Mrs. Smith's pie. Even when I showed the judge the Mrs. Smith's box, pulled from the trash, he was not swayed. True, the first year we under-cooked the pie and the second year we overcompensated for it (translation: even the pumpkin was burned). But to lose to a store-bought pie was humiliating. I vowed that this year things would be different. We had a new recipe and the cooking time down to the second. We were ready!

As dinner approached, my assistants and I began to get nervous. What if we used too much nutmeg? What if it wasn't edible? What if Cindy brings a Sara Lee pie this year? We decided not to leave our fate to the hands of chance.

Our plan was glorious in its simplicity: we'd bribe the judge and sabotage the competition. When he arrived, we quietly slipped him a few dollars for his trouble.

"Perhaps this will help you decide," I whispered, as I tucked two dollars into the pocket of his suit.

While everyone was eating, I slipped away and placed little paper roaches on top of the three other pies in the contest. Mr. Minter would uncover three pies that would make him sick, leaving only my pie as the winner. It would be no contest and the golden turkey would be mine!

The ambiance was perfect. The room looked and smelled of Thanksgiving. The dinner was delicious and it was finally time for the unveiling of the pies and the taste test.

One by one the pies were brought forth and set before Mr. Minter. Since the previous year's winners went first, I knew my pie would be the last one, which fit per-fectly into my plan. Mr. Minter uncovered the first pie. I think it safe to say he was disgusted. By the second pie he was repulsed and by the third, nauseated. He even looked a little green. To my delight the paper roaches had absorbed some of the condensation from atop the pie and enlarged to an even uglier size and shape.

I couldn't lose. My pie was next. I saw a smile purse Mr. Minter's lips as he patted his pocket containing the money. I knew we had him. The golden turkey would sit in my classroom for the next year; I had the spot already picked out.

Eager to make an impression, I had decided my pie should make an entrance. Lenny2 would bring it to the front of the room and place it in front of Mr. Minter for the unveiling. We put a Michael Jackson record on the player and Lenny started forward from the back of the room. As fate would have it, along the way he stopped at the other Lenny's desk to look at a cardboard black cat still hanging from the ceiling after Halloween. This was not in my script, but it seemed to add to the anticipation of the moment. Unfortunately, I hadn't planned in the extra time. Michael Jackson finished his first slow and melodious pie song and the second song started playing. When the loud and infectious beat of the song kicked in, Lenny the dancer erupted from his seat, as he often did when the music grabbed him.

Physics was a subject I steered clear of with my students, but we learned that day that two people couldn't occupy the same space at the same time.

As Lenny exploded from his seat he collided with Lenny2 carrying the pie.

SMACK! The two Lennys hit and my pie, my glorious dessert, my ticket to the golden turkey, launched skyward and began to spin. Over and over it turned in a surreal pirouette as it went higher and higher and then started falling to the floor. As it spun around in slow motion the aluminum foil slipped away revealing what, I still feel, was the best pie that day. I was hoping Mr. Minter was watching.

SPLAT! My beautiful pie hit face down on the carpeted floor of the room. This being a creamier pie that most, when it hit it spread out in a huge lump on the floor.

Dancing Lenny was too busy bobbing up and down to even notice what was happening.

"Oh shit!" the other Lenny said, as he looked at the pie on the floor. I had never heard him speak with more clarity. It was as if his palate was cured for one brief moment in time. As I looked around the room I knew everyone else had understood him too.

"It's OK Lenny," I said, running over to save what I could of a bad situation and totally ignoring his language. After all, he had just said what I was thinking.

"It was an accident. Besides, it's not a total loss."

I scooped up what I could from the carpet and molded it back into a pie shape then set it on a plate in front of Mr. Minter. It was bruised and full of hair and dirt but I was still counting on the bribe, although I wished I had come up with a little more than two dollars.

Unfortunately, once the other teachers removed the paper roaches from their pies, mine didn't look as appealing. They only had to remove a paper roach; I had to remove tiny pieces of hair, dirt and carpet fibers. As I had predicted, it was no contest.

"I'm sorry," Mr. Minter said, shaking my hand and returning the money as he left for the day.

"It's OK," I said, accepting my defeat gracefully. "We'll see you next year, right?"

"Oh, yes," he said, patting his stomach. "I wouldn't miss it."

I was fairly confident that Darlene's mother would love her haircut and I was certain my pie would win the contest. Yet before me sat a bald young girl and a splattered pie.

It wasn't difficult for me to cope with these incidents, because I was used to change and disappointment. But my students were so structured in their thinking that they had a difficult time contending with the daily upsets that are a part of life. As I scraped the remainder of my pie out of the carpet, a thought hit me. I should be doing more to prepare my students for the changes that are inevitable in their lives.

While it is impossible to anticipate every specific change that might ever occur, we can prepare them for change in general. I wanted to help them learn to cope with the unexpected and learn that the world doesn't end when their routine does.

From that day forward I structured change into my program. I changed the set up of the room, what we were doing, how and when we did it—anything to help my students become more comfortable with variations in their lives.

Not only did I structure change but I started welcoming, instead of resisting, those abrupt and unforeseen changes that occur as we live our lives from day to day. A bus that failed to show, a sudden rainstorm that drenched us on our walk, an unexpected visitor—all had a place in our lives and didn't need to cause too much anxiety.

That Thanksgiving holiday I gave thanks to Darlene and the two Lennys for helping me remember that there are no guarantees. Despite our best plans and efforts, sometimes life turns in another direction. I thanked them for reminding me that unpredictability is all that's predictable.

As it turned out, it was an auspicious time to learn that lesson. It would soon come in handy....

Chapter Eighteen

You Never Know Until You Try

*T*he winds of educational change were blowing across the nation; Florida was no exception.

In Ohio, I taught at a school where handicapped and non-handicapped students were integrated, at least to a degree; they were all housed in the same building. In Florida, I was teaching at a center filled only with handicapped students.

Later that same school year, Mr. Minter reported that the county was going to move a class of handicapped students out of Nina and into Osceola Middle School, in nearby Largo, beginning with the next school year. They had chosen autistic students for the experiment. I volunteered. Since there were no other takers, my class was selected, at least those students whose parents would agree to make this initial step.

I have often wondered about my decision. I made it quickly and without much deliberation, as I was confident that I could be successful. After all, handling new challenges was a part of my nature.

Nina had been a safe haven for my students and me. We were surrounded by other students with handicaps and by teachers like me, who valued them. For the most part, our environment had been nourishing, accepting and relatively harmless. While my class had been part of a regular school in Ohio, that was eons ago.

Integrating disabled students with nondisabled students had never been attempted before in our county. The idea was met with opposition and apprehension. None of us knew what to expect. Why did I see it as an adventure and not an accident waiting to happen? Perhaps if I had thought it through more carefully, I would have been just as uneasy.

But I wasn't. So we began the adventure by asking parents to allow their sons and daughters to leave the security of Nina for the unfamiliar world of a middle school. I assured them that I would do my best to keep their loved ones safe and happy. Eight parents accepted the challenge and we were confirmed to go.

When the staff at Osceola Middle School heard an autistic class was coming, some of the teachers were anxious and uncertain. I spent many of the days leading up to my students' arrival trying to allay these fears. If the teachers accepted my class, I knew their students would not be too far behind.

As I walked the halls of Osceola that first week, I realized it was I who should have been anxious. I had taught at Nina for a number of years; the students I remembered from regular school had changed in my absence. It was like emerging from a time warp. While there were many good students, much to my chagrin I noticed too many students were rude and disrespectful to everyone. I wasn't ready for that. But we were here and we would experience it together. The eyes of many people were watching us, both those who knew we would fail and those who knew we wouldn't. There was no turning back.

As I waited for my students' bus that first day, I learned my first real-world lesson. At Nina, the transition of students from bus to school is easygoing and orderly. At Osceola, the buses unloaded students all at once and everywhere. One minute there was quiet; the next it was as if someone opened the doors to a concert. As my assistant, Debbie, and I played bumper people, I remembered my promise to the parents to keep their sons and daughters safe, secure and happy. This was not a responsibility I took lightly and I was a little concerned. Not only had I been isolated at Nina, so had my students. This was as much a culture shock for them as for me. In retrospect, they handled it much better than did I.

We spent the morning acclimating to our new surroundings, finding the cafeteria, the gym, locating the restrooms, etc. Initially, my only concession to safety was not allowing my students to be in the hallways during the change of class. Entering the hallway at this time was like trying to leave pit row and reenter the Daytona 500. All around people were moving fast, bumping each other, and in very close proximity. Trying to change directions could be fatal.

We made it through the first four periods of our day and were feeling pretty good about ourselves when the bell rang for fifth period.

"OK everyone, it's time for PE," I said innocently. "Line up and we'll walk you to the gym."

My students obliged all too well. However, unbeknownst to us, Chris, the line leader, stepped out into the hall and the others followed like lemmings. One by one they unwittingly became members of a stampede.

Debbie was the first to notice the problem.

"Jim!" she screamed. "They're gone!"

I rushed to the door just in time to see the last of my students, the same students whose safety I had guaranteed to their parents, get swept up in a tidal wave of teenagers.

Luckily an unrelated event from the previous summer at Nina proved to be a Godsend. Chris, a student I had previously taught but who had moved away, rejoined our class at Osceola. He was a thin boy with blond hair, freckles and a great smile. He loved noises, any kind of noises. If he heard a burp, he'd laugh. If he heard a tractor or a lawn mower, he'd want to see it. By far his most favorite noise, the one that sent him into exhilaration, was a sneeze. When someone sneezed Chris would slump over, hold his mouth, turn bright red, smile broadly, then be overcome with laughter. It was genuine, unsolicited laughter and it was infectious. It was not a behavior we even tried to change, as it was one of his most endearing qualities.

Chris was also a human chameleon. He was extremely observant and would easily take on the characteristics of other students. If a student in my class had a nasty habit and received any attention at all for it, Chris developed the same habit. (He particularly loved the bad habits.) He also possessed an obstinate streak. Although his language was severely limited, if he wasn't in the mood to work, he still got his message across. He would scrunch up his lips, shake his head and refuse to move. On the infrequent occasion when we pushed him farther than he could handle, he would bite his fingers and flap his hands.

The new Chris had grown into a tall young man. He looked the same but now stood 6'2" tall; it was a glorious 6'2".

"What are we going to do?" Debbie asked, as the wave of students engulfed my class.

"Follow Chris," I said.

"Chris?" Debbie sighed in frustration.

"Sure, he's the tallest person in the school. Look for his head and follow it."

"I see him!" Debbie said.

We looked and, sure enough, there was Chris' blond head bobbing up and down high above the other students. He was smiling and happy, oblivious to the two ranting and raving lunatics trying desperately to follow him.

Debbie took off first and I followed, pushing Ethan. As I looked ahead, Chris was having a great time and Ethan seemed to be enjoying the chaotic ride through all the people. It was nice to know someone was finding this amusing.

We followed Chris' bouncing head as it flowed along the river of people. It was like chasing a runaway raft down the rapids. It bobbed from our room to the end of the hallway, out the door, then across the courtyard. He turned into another building, went down the hall and finally turned into a room at the end of the hall, where we caught up with him.

"I don't believe it," Debbie said, counting our students. "We didn't lose a single one. They all made it. They all made it."

They all must have followed Chris' head.

Debbie and I looked at each other.

"Boy, were we lucky," she said, as we walked the class to PE.

"Yeah, but you know something?" I said, patting Chris on the back. "Maybe it was a good thing after all."

Debbie stopped and turned toward me, as a look of confusion overtook her face.

"Come on everyone. It's time for PE," I said with a smile.

Jack also made the move to Osceola. He quickly developed a relationship with Chris, their common bond being sound. I hadn't realized that Jack had an interest in sounds until Chris arrived. They would laugh together when they heard any odd sound. They would make little sounds back and forth to one another and laugh and laugh and laugh. It was their own basis for a friendship and it lasted as long as they were classmates.

As we were gathering students each morning, Chris and Jack would be laughing at the sounds of the brakes on the buses. Then, on the way to the classroom they'd play their little sound game. One day, while watching them, I realized they weren't following me at all, but were walking in the direction of the classroom, totally engrossed in their game. It made me question whether or not they needed me to meet them every day. Perhaps they could make it to the room on their own. I decided to give it a whirl.

Before they left school that afternoon I told the class that in the morning, they were to come to the room on their own. I waited for their objections, but none came. They didn't even seem too concerned. Perhaps they hadn't understood what I said.

To ease my worry, the next morning I surreptitiously stationed myself behind a pillar away from the buses, but with a clear view of the scene. As the morning frenzy began, I watched and waited. It was difficult to locate each of my students in the rush of humanity, but it was too late to turn back now. I waited and waited. Finally, as I cowered behind the post, I felt a tap on my shoulder. It was Jack, along with Larry, Pat, Chris, Martin and Larue.

"Mr. Yerman," he asked, "are you going to the room now?"

It seems they were on their way to the room when they spotted me and came over to see if I needed any help.

"Ah—yes, sure Jack," I said, straightening my shirt and attempting to look like I knew what I was doing. "I'll follow you."

As we walked I couldn't figure out how these five students had beaten my surveillance. Good thing I was never in the military.

So many of my student's lives are planned for them, by well-meaning parents, family and teachers. Theirs is a safe and supervised world, where they don't have to make many decisions or judgments. Those first few weeks at Osceola made me realize that my students deserved more than that. They deserved the chance to make choices. We owed them the opportunity to make mistakes and try again. After all, Thomas Edison invented the light bulb only after numerous attempts failed.

It's our fear of mistakes that usually gets in the way. We don't know if our students or our children will succeed or fail until we let them try. However, all students, no matter their capacity, need the same freedom to make choices and the opportunity to learn from them.

Our lives are filled with moments of decision. The choices we make can, and often do, determine not only our lives, but those of the people we influence. I have never regretted my decision to move our program from Nina to Osceola, as it taught me the value of independence and enabled me to empower my students a little more.

In the end, closing the door to our secure and safe environment at Nina opened up a whole new world for my students and for me. Decisions are like that; you never know how far they can take you. In the end, so what if some of them are mistakes? We only lose when we stay stagnant.

Chapter Nineteen
The Chance to Belong

I was in a unique and wonderful position at Osceola. This new home for our class furnished my students with many opportunities to learn from their non-handicapped peers. I also believed it was an opportunity for other students to learn from mine. Since at that time, autism was still a little known disability, it frightened many people, including staff, students and school personnel. As a one-man mission to promote understanding, I started visiting classrooms to discuss my students' challenges and unique abilities. Part of my presentation was to introduce the students to members of my class.

The first class I spoke to was 35 students; they stopped me dead in my tracks. I had never seen a class of students this size. Since I started teaching, my classes had been eight to twelve students, with one or two assistants. Of course, I had spoken in front of larger groups of students at Kent State, but they were my peers, not middle school kids. I felt alone and self-conscious standing in front of that class. Although I had prepared and knew what I was going to say, I froze.

After what seemed like an eternity, a girl in the front row asked me what autism was. It was the jump-start I needed. After explaining the disability and answering a few more questions, I brought in my class and they sat among the other students. One by one I introduced them to the class and talked to them for a while. I wanted the regular students to see what a difficult time many of them had with language and what a profound effect it had on their lives. I also wanted them to hear about the things they liked and the activities they enjoyed, to highlight the similarities that existed between them.

As Lenny talked about his interest in boats the tension lifted in the room. Jack talked about his love of music, (he was a Peter, Paul, and Mary groupie—very "in" at that time), and Gus wowed them with his knowledge of game shows. Everyone relaxed a little more. But the two biggest hits that day were Martin and Ethan.

Martin was a wonderful young man. He stood 5'5" tall and was a very round 250 pounds. He had black curly hair cropped close to his dark skin. He was born with his feet turned outward, so much so that when he stood up his heels touched and his feet would form a straight line. There was a way to correct this abnormality, but his parents decided to try prayer instead. It didn't work and now he looked like an overweight Charlie Chaplin. At his weight it was a wonder he could stand at all, but he had incredible balance. When he wanted, he could run very fast. Martin loved to draw and write, but by far his best attribute was his memory.

He knew vegetables. He kept a notebook filled with vegetables he had drawn and labeled. It contained page after page of eggplant, summer squash, zucchini, etc. If there was a vegetable grown anywhere in the world, Martin had catalogued it.

He also knew counties. One of his favorite activities was drawing the state of Florida, then outlining every county in the state. When he went to the board and drew a precise map of Florida, the class fell silent. When he drew in every county and began labeling them the students were duly impressed.

Martin also knew state capitals. If I said a state, he would immediately respond with the capital.

"Alabama," I'd say.

"Montgomery," was his response.

"Ohio."

"Columbus."

There was no stumping him. Some of the students tried their luck.

"Utah."

"Salt Lake City."

"Montana."

"Helena."

"Pennsylvania."

"Harrisburg."

When he finally sat down it was to a thunderous applause.

Martin's ability with state capitals lead to an astonishing bit of socialization throughout his tenure at Osceola Middle School. Students would come by, stick their heads in the door to our room and name a state. Without looking up from his vegetable book, Martin would blurt out the correct capital. Day in and day out it was a way for the regular students to interact with him; everyone seemed to enjoy the exchange.

One by one the rest of my class came to the front of the room. We talked and laughed and taught them more about autism. The other students eagerly asked them questions and a continuous dialogue unfolded. It seemed that many of the students had handicapped people in their lives; it became a common link between them.

Ethan was the last student to be introduced to the class. Because he was in the wheel chair, he generated the most questions. The students seemed genuinely interested in his muscular dystrophy but they were especially interested in his wheel chair. From the time Ethan was confined to a wheel chair his mom had tried to get him an electric one but failed. As luck would have it, he had received one that very week. It fascinated the other students. Ethan had already become somewhat adept at using it and he loved it. It gave him a certain amount of independence: no longer did he need to be pushed from place to place.

One of the students asked what it was like to ride in his wheel chair. As we had brought Ethan's hoist with us—a device that suspended him in the air—we gave the students, including mine, turns riding in his wheelchair. Even their teacher took a turn. Everyone had a chance to experience a little bit of Ethan's world. Then we settled Ethan back in the chair and he showed how proficient he had already become with the controls.

Our presentations proved successful in creating a spirit of unity between the autism class and the other students. I continued introducing my students to any and all classes that would give us the opportunity, and I still do so today.

Although this scheduled, structured form of public awareness was valuable and needed, it was the everyday events at Osceola that taught us the most.

Only one Lenny made the move with us to our new school, and this Lenny was very social. He would try to talk to anyone who would listen—classmate, teacher or complete stranger. Despite us trying to teach him to approach only people he knew, Lenny was stubborn and independent. He also had somehow learned to use his speech impediment to his advantage.

I was in my room one morning, awaiting the arrival of our group. It was about a week into their independence in getting there on their own.

"Mr. Yerman!" came a cry at my door from a female student. "Mr. Yerman, I need your help."

"Come on in," I said, relishing the opportunity to help others deal with my students. "What can I do for you?"

Then another girl ran to my doorway.

"Mr. Yerman, you've got to do something."

"Mr. Yerman!" another girl screamed into my room.

Before I had a chance to think, six girls were standing in my room with mixtures of exasperation and anger on their faces.

After calming everyone down, I was able to piece together what was causing such an uproar. Their complaints were all the same: Lenny had kissed them.

"I'll take care of this," I told them, as Lenny walked into the room.

The girls all moved behind me, making sure I was between them and Don Juan.

I asked Lenny what had happened. It seems he wanted to meet some girls. Having never done this before, he came up with a novel approach. He would spot a likely prospect and walk up to her.

"Hello, do you like me?" he would ask.

Since this came out in his unintelligible nasal way, the girl would say something like, "I'm sorry, what did you say?" and lean in closer, hoping this would help her understand.

"I said, do you like me?" Lenny would repeat, causing still more confusion.

After a few of these questions most girls—or at least six I knew of—answered "yes" hoping it was the right answer.

Of course, to Lenny it was, his green light to proceed with a kiss on the cheek. (I couldn't help but admire Lenny's technique and wished I had tried it in school.)

We discussed what behaviors were appropriate and those that were not. Since the six victims were still in the room, I had Lenny apologize to each of them and we started all over again. Lenny asked each girl her name and told her his name. Then we all agreed, although Lenny somewhat begrudgingly, that from now on there would be no more kissing.

I had never dreamed that teaching the correct way to meet women would be part of my job or that "no kissing" would become one of my class rules.

A short time after the kissing incident, a new student arrived on our doorstep.

"Mr. Yerman," a voice boomed from the PA system.

"Yes," I responded.

"Mr. Yerman, we think we have one of your students up here. Her bus just arrived."

"No, I don't think so," I returned. "Her bus doesn't arrive for another half hour."

There was a pause and I could here mumbling.

"We think it must have come early."

"What makes you think so?" I asked.

"She's running around in circles, flapping her hands and asking to sleep on the carpet."

"I'll be right up."

Jenny was a round 14-year-old girl. She had a thick head of brown curly hair and a cherubic smile. Her eyes were blue, one clear and alert and one that remained continuously cloudy. She had very limited vision in her left eye and none in her right. She stood about four feet tall and her arms were noticeably shorter than they should have been. She didn't understand much language, evidenced by her echolalia.

Echolalia is a condition where a person repeats what he or she has heard, either immediately prior, or at some point in the past. It is a very limited form of communication in some people with autism. For instance, if you asked, "How are you today?" Jenny would repeat "How are you today?" If you followed with, "No Jenny, say I'm fine." so would she. It's like the times you put a dollar bill into a vending machine and it spits it back out. The dollar goes in, cannot be processed, and comes back out. That's how Jenny handled language; if she didn't understand it, she'd spit it back out.

Despite her numerous physical and cognitive problems. Jenny was a happy child. She loved to laugh and show her excitement by flitting her hands at her chest or leaning back in her chair with her hands out to the sides and fluttering like a hummingbird over a flower. When she was extremely happy she would spin faster and faster in one spot, start flapping and say, "Great Balls of Fire." She could spin faster than anyone I had ever seen, then stop and walk away with no apparent dizziness.

Jenny loved music. She had many of her favorite verses, as well as lines and remarks she had heard over the years, stored inside her head. In addition to her spontaneous echolalia, Jenny had delayed echolalia. She would remember and repeat entire sentences she had heard yesterday, last week, or years ago. Many of these one-liners came out at times when they made no sense to us. But they must have had some meaning to her.

I was never sure what was going to come bursting from her lips, or when.

"I want the movie rights, Yerman," she might say as we were walking down the hallway. She always called me by my last name only, a habit I found endearing.

"We're gonna get married, Yerman," would escape from her lips another time.

"I want to break up, Yerman," would come out another time.

Usually these unrehearsed and unexpected expressions were a source of entertainment for my assistants and myself. Even Jenny seemed to know she was kidding around, as she would flap and laugh when she said something outrageous. They were always funny, sometimes hilarious, but occasionally downright embarrassing.

I was giving my autism awareness talk to a class of students one day. It was Jenny's turn to come forward. I believe my students have always enjoyed their 15 minutes of fame; Jenny was no different.

She flitted to the front of the room. I had just finished describing her echolalia and was demonstrating it to the class.

"Jenny," I said. "Can you say hello to the class?"
Her usual response was to repeat the question.
"Hi" she said, waving to everyone.
"Good job," I said. "What did you do last night?"
Jenny's face lit up.
"I went to 7-11."
Jenny's father takes her to 7-11, a convenience store, for a soda.

"Great, what did you get there?"

"A Pepsi," she answered.

I was experiencing an odd combination of feelings. We were having more of a conversation than we had ever had together, which made me glad. But I knew the class was waiting to see her echolalia.

I'm not sure, but I think she was enjoying my little predicament. After every response she would flit and laugh. The class seemed to be enjoying her.

"OK Jenny," I said, patting her on the shoulder. "Why don't you go back to your seat now."

Jenny looked up at me and smiled—a smile I had seen on two other little girls' faces in my teaching career. Although the class didn't know it, I was beginning to get a little nervous. I had seen that smile before from Linda and Darlene.

Jenny cocked her head back, smiled sweetly, flitted her hands and said,

"Why don't we do it in the road, Yerman?"

I winced, then closed my eyes. When I opened them unfortunately I was still standing in front of a classroom filled with seventh grade students.

Jenny's statement settled like a cloud over the group. As she went off flitting and laughing, I explained again about delayed echolalia.

I'm not sure anyone believed me.

Osceola was an ocean of possibilities. Students, both mine and those in the other classes, were daily teaching me new lessons. I could feel myself growing both as a person and a teacher, and believed that the students were growing and learning as well.

One lesson we all learned was not to fear the unknown. My students became more comfortable in their new environment as they learned more about it. The teachers and students at Osceola learned that people with autism were not be feared just because they were a little different. More importantly, they learned that despite the differences, they all had some things in common. Given the opportunity, acceptance and even friendships were possible.

Yes, ours was a unique and wonderful position to be in at Osceola Middle School.

Chapter Twenty

Watch Out for Bumps

*T*he first year at Osceola was filled with bumps. We were in uncharted territory and never knew what was going to happen next. I responded by learning to think on my feet, be more flexible and roll with the punches. My students, on the other hand, needed some help with the transition.

Martin was not much of a conversationalist. When he did talk, it was in a whisper. The only two times he spoke with any volume were when he was spouting off state capitals and when he was frustrated. When he did not understand a problem or a question he would, in a resounding tone, begin pointing to and labeling things in the room.

"There's the carpet," he'd say, pointing to the floor.

"There's the wall."

"There's the door."

This was his way of dealing with change and frustration. To help communicate more fully with others, we tried teaching him more appropriate sentences, like "I don't know", or "I am angry" or "I'm confused." Try as we might, when Martin got anxious, he returned to his labeling.

Certainly there are worse ways of dealing with anxiety.

Paul had made the trip from Nina to Osceola with us and Kelly joined us during that first year.

Paul was a tall, thin young man with a slight wave to his ebony hair. He had dark eyes, set deeply into his long face. He understood much of what he heard and could talk, although he was difficult to understand. Paul was rigid. He liked schedules to be followed with no variation. This internal need for structure was a constant source of torment for him.

We taught Paul how to open his gym locker and, when we thought he was ready, let him dress by himself for PE. Given his need for a schedule to follow, we set up an easy one: open the locker, get dressed, close the locker then go outside and sit in line for roll call. We stressed to Paul that once his locker was closed he was to go outside.

The first day he was on his own Mr. Popejoy, his PE coach, and I waited in his office until Paul had enough time to go through his routine and get seated in the line.

"Mr. Popejoy," a student said, sticking his head into the office, "I think you'd better come see this."

"Where?" Mr. Popejoy said.

"Outside. Outside in the line. I think you'd better come."

We walked outside to see the students sitting in their lines on the cement. Instantly we noticed that everyone, except my students, was either laughing or trying not to laugh. Snickers and chuckles and murmurs were circulating throughout the students. As we followed the flow of chatter our eyes came to rest on the cause of all the commotion. Paul was sitting in his correct spot in line, obviously upset. His eyes were squinting, his forehead was tense, and he was swinging his head back and forth in a constant pendulum-like motion. Further observation on our part showed that he was sitting there in only his underwear. That's right; only a pair of BVDs separated Paul from his birthday suit, a fact highlighted by the girls who were part of the coed PE class.

"Paul," I said. "Why don't you come with me."

I was determined to find out what went wrong. How did we get from total independence to a Chippendale dancer?

After a short discussion, I realized that Paul's rigidity in following his schedule was his undoing.

He opened his locker and undressed without a problem. The unforeseen element of our plan happened next. Apparently one of the other students inadvertently hit his locker door and it closed. Our training and Paul's inflexibility kicked in. With his locker closed, the next step was to go outside and sit in line. So he did.

Paul knew not to go outside in his underwear, but he was unable to think through any alternatives. I reviewed the procedure with him and we practiced various other scenarios to help him learn what to do in each situation. Occasionally throughout the school year we reviewed them with him. Fortunately for all of us, especially Paul, this was the only incident he faced—of this kind.

Of course, there would be other incidents.

We stressed to Paul that when confused, he needed to ask for help. He just needed to speak up.

Kelly, another student in our class, could have used some of Paul's discretion.

Kelly was a 15-year-old girl with short curly black hair. She wore thick, dark-rimmed glasses covering dark brown eyes. She loved make-up of any kind and preferred doing her nails to any other activity. Kelly, like Paul, was also somewhat resistant to change. Her reaction, however, was to swear like a sailor.

For the most part Kelly was a quiet, reserved young lady, impeccably dressed and manicured. I knew she liked to look good but I didn't know how much she needed to look good until the day she broke a nail.

She was working on a math worksheet. The class was quiet and everything seemed to be going along just fine. Suddenly Kelly blurted out some profanity, then another and another and before I could get to her seat, the room was echoing obscenities. I looked around at my other students. Many times my students remain oblivious to the events going on around them. Usually I am not happy with this oblivion; today I was hoping for it.

"Mr. Yerman, did you hear what Kelly said?" Lenny asked nasally. "She said—"

"Lenny, stop!" I yelled. I had heard it once. I didn't need to hear it again, nasally or not.

As I arrived at Kelly's desk she was readying for another round.

"Kelly, what's the matter?" I asked.

"Look at this damn nail," she said. "I broke this fu—"

"Kelly, Kelly," I said. "Let's try to talk a little nicer, shall we? Now, what can we do about your nail?"

"Not a God Damn—"

"Kelly," I said sternly. "Stop it!"

Kelly looked at me and tightened her lips.

We discussed a better way to handle her disappointment and replayed the entire scene to help her learn how to cope. The plan was for her to get a pencil and a piece of paper and write down what she was angry about and, if she felt she had to swear, to swear in writing.

Going back over situations and helping my students practice better ways of handling problems is a useful technique. However, it's difficult to determine if it's effective. If the behavior recurs, it was not effective. If it does not, perhaps the circumstances were not similar enough. At any rate, time would tell if Paul and Kelly learned anything from the technique.

Paul's rigidity manifested itself in other peculiar ways. Even though we didn't physically change classrooms, my students would follow the same schedule as the rest of the middle school. This meant when the bell rang ending first period we would also end our activity. One morning I was running behind in our lesson. As I wanted to finish what we were doing, I decided to keep teaching past the bell.

I was so engrossed in the lesson that I didn't notice Paul's rising anxiety. When he stood up and turned his desk over on the floor, I took notice. It was odd that he didn't throw it, but gently lifted it and set it on the floor. It barely made a sound as he placed it there. Although he was angry and frustrated, he still managed to retain a semblance of gentleness.

I looked at Paul. His tongue was slightly visible out of the corner of his mouth and his head was swaying back and forth.

"Paul, what's the matter?" I asked.

He looked around, then ran to the front of the room and began turning over everyone's desk with the same tenderness he exercised on his own.

Since I was as stunned as anyone, this went on for a few minutes. It was amazing that the rest of the students didn't seem to notice Paul at all. As he turned over their desks they continued sitting there, as if nothing had happened. Unfortunately, I let it go on a little too long. He reached Kelly's desk and proceeded to turn it over, upsetting the meticulous arrangement of her materials.

I was relatively sure by now that my plan for Paul's frustration management was a failure. Now we would see how Kelly's anger management strategy would hold up to scrutiny.

She jumped up from her seat.

"Holy shit!" she exclaimed, instead of going to get a pencil and paper and writing down her feelings. This was followed by a slew of words, some of which even I didn't know.

People began running into my room to see if I needed any help. I didn't know if I did, because I still wasn't sure what to do. My eyes ping ponged from Paul to Kelly and back to Paul. It was an endless tennis match of the absurd and I, as the referee, had lost control.

Just when I thought it couldn't get any worse, Paul toppled Martin's desk and an absurd rhythm began.

THUMP!

"Shit!"

"There's the carpet."

THUMP!

"Mother F—"

"There's the window."

THUMP!

"God Dam—"

"There's the pencil sharpener."

All this commotion became just too much for Jenny. She stood up, and began spinning wildly, yelling "Great Balls Of Fire."

It was a surreal orchestration that the non-paying public gathered in my doorway seemed to be enjoying a little too much. It was not the type of "togetherness" that I had in mind when we came to Osceola.

When things were finally under control, I took the three main characters aside and we rehearsed correct procedures for the next time havoc struck. Only time would tell.

I HAD been taking my class to work in a warehouse near our school. I like going into the community. Not only does it increase opportunities for teaching and learning, it gives us chance after chance to deal with the everyday changes that occur in life.

One day, after arriving at the warehouse, I neglected to buckle Ethan into his wheel chair. As we all entered the warehouse, his wheelchair stopped abruptly on the door frame; Ethan did not.

"No-o-o-o," he yelled, as he was ejected from his seat.

I was trapped behind the chair and could not reach his falling body.

He hit the cement, head first.

I threw the wheel chair out of the way, ran to Ethan and turned him over. I didn't know what I was going to see. I just wanted him to be alive.

"Mr. Yerman, head hurt," was all he could muster as I turned him over.

I was so glad he was alive that I hugged him to my chest. With blood gushing out of Ethan's head and covering both of us, Paul walked up to me. True to form, he said, "Mr. Yerman, it's time to get to work."

Although it took 11 stitches, we all survived this accident. When we returned to school, we discussed what had happened and what to do the next time I forgot to strap Ethan in.

The need for sameness in an ever-changing world makes it difficult for some of my students to cope with life's inconstancy. I am sure the emotional pain they feel when their order is upset is as real as was Ethan's physical pain. Their frustration manifests itself in myriad ways, some appropriate and some not so appropriate.

So we discuss, we rehash events, and we take the time to replay these situations over and over. We try to anticipate new things that might happen to throw a wrench into our procedure. All with the hope of helping everyone survive a little easier in the future. While we certainly can't anticipate every predicament that might ever happen, the practice helps ease some of the tension my students feel when life does not go according to their plan.

When bumps occur along the unpredictable road of life, I help my students over them. Together we climb over each bump one at a time as they endeavor to cope with their autism—a bump from which they will never fully recover.

Chapter Twenty-One
The View from Here is Wonderful

*I*t's difficult to be a true non-conformist. Groups come and go, all trying to break away from the status quo. Within the group the members dress alike, have similar hairstyles, and repeat the same rhetoric, all in the name of individuality.

Although none of us wants to be seen as a clone, I believe we all make an effort to conform. It's part of our existence as social human beings to want to fit it and belong to a group. The sense of unity that groups provide make us feel good about ourselves and feel secure in life.

Many autistic people do not feel the urge to conform to our social rules, however. They do not seem to care how they look or act. Although they may share characteristics with others, they are truly individualists, without ever striving to be.

Back at Nina, I didn't worry much about what other people thought about my students. We were a special education center, all kindred spirits. The atmosphere was one of acceptance and understanding. When we moved to Osceola, the walls of our classroom expanded to include any place we happened to be. Whether we were in the hallways, the cafeteria or the community, I started becoming acutely aware of other people's perceptions and reactions to my students. There, we were no longer all kindred spirits. My students were merely a part of the whole and for the most part, it seemed we were on the outside, looking in.

Within the global classroom of life, reactions to my students were mixed, as were our reactions to the rest of the world.

AFTER Lenny's Casanova impersonation, he settled in and became quite the gentleman. I was happy that he had learned his lesson and, to my relief, he acted appropriately with the female students at Osceola.

One Saturday I received a call from Lenny's mother; she was in tears. She had allowed Lenny to play, unsupervised, in a park near their home. The police had just brought him home.

It seems Lenny had noticed the other families around him. He realized that while he was playing by himself, he saw fathers and mothers playing with their sons and daughters. He saw brothers playing with their sisters and he realized he did not have a sister. He had a brother, but no sister. He thought it might be nice to have a sister and thought that certainly his mother and father would like it, too. So he tried to remedy the situation. He spotted a family nearby, walked over, took the girl by the arm and began pulling. The girl screamed, the mother screamed, Lenny said some things no one understood and the police were summoned.

The police were able to determine where Lenny lived and took him home.

"He's never done anything like this before," his mother told the police officer, as he handed Lenny over to her. "And I assure you, he will never do it again."

"Please make sure he doesn't." The officer's tone was stern.

When Lenny's mother asked him what had happened his response was simple and succinct.

"I wanted a sister," he said, wondering what all the fuss was about.

Lenny didn't understand how the people around him would react. He didn't stop to think that they might be shocked and angry.

Back in school on Monday, we talked about families. I asked Lenny how he would feel if he was taken away from his mom and dad. He seemed to get the message and never went sister hunting again.

Sometimes we were the ones shocked by people's reactions.

My class was in a grocery store one day, walking as a group looking for items and prices. I noticed an elderly couple shopping nearby.

"Those people ought to stay where they belong," the elderly man said loudly as we passed them.

My students ignored him as they are wont to do. I stopped in the aisle, startled at his reaction.

"I can't believe they let them in the store," he continued, loud enough for anyone to hear.

I looked back and our eyes met. His were filled with anger yet I couldn't fathom why. Given my one-man mission to help the world understand autism, I asked Debbie to watch the class and I went over to talk to him. I was sure that once I spoke with him he would change his attitude.

"Excuse me," I said politely. "Do you have a problem with us?"

"You bet I do," he shot back. "Where do you get off bringing those kind of people into this store? They don't belong here."

"What kind of people are you talking about, sir?" I asked calmly.

"You know darn well what I mean. We come into this store every week and we don't want to be disturbed by— by— by those idiots."

He pointed at my class.

I remained calm, realizing it wouldn't help to stoop to his level.

"Sir, they are autistic. That means—"

"I don't care what you call them. They don't belong in a public place."

"But sir," I implored, "if you'll let me explain."

"I don't have to listen. If you don't get those people out of this store I am going to the manager."

"Listen, you old coot," I said, quickly lowering myself way past his level. "My students were born the way they are; what's your excuse? We have just as much right to be here as you do and we're not leaving just because you're an ignoramus. Go ahead and tell the manager. See if I care."

The manager knew we were there and had no objection.

I turned and walked away.

"And another thing," I said, turning back toward him, "the only idiot in this store is you."

I'm surprised I didn't stick out my tongue or say something rude about his mother!

It was a good lesson for me to realize that the whole world did not think of my students with the same fondness as did I. It helped me understand that not only had my students been isolated from the world, but the world had been isolated from them. It certainly bolstered my desire to keep trying. I still think, even today, that we have a lot to offer and learn from one another.

CHANGING public opinion about people with autism even reached to our principal, Mr. Johnson.

Mr. Johnson was not a nice man but, for the most part, since he enjoyed the publicity my class gave him, he left us alone. It was great for his professional image to have the first autistic class in a regular school in our county. He never stopped milking it for all it was worth. He was constantly bringing visitors into my room to show off the class. However, when observers weren't around, we never saw him. He acted like a politician running for office when spectators were present.

The door would burst open.

"Hi, Mr. Yerman," he would say, introducing me to the people with him.

"Hi, Bob, how are you today?" he'd say, shaking one of my student's hands.

"Samantha, good to see you."

"And here is Billy."

"Hi, Terry."

On and on he'd go until he had spoken to and introduced everyone in the room. Then he would usher his followers out and they were gone. I am sure his entourage was impressed but there was one minor problem. Except for me, he never got anyone's name correct, even Debbie, my assistant. It was all an act. I often wished there was some way to teach him a lesson. Then one day, Kelly did it for me.

"Good morning, everyone," Mr. Johnson said, barging into the room with a slew of people in tow.

He began his normal charade.

"Hi Bob," he said, shaking Lenny's hand.

"I'm not Bob," Lenny said unintelligibly.

"Hi Tim," he said shaking Jack's hand.

Once again his little act was working.

"Hi Sally," he said, as he got to Kelly, who was new to us since the last time Mr. Johnson visited.

"That's not my fucking name," Kelly snapped back.

This was one time I was glad my anger management program was such a failure.

Mr. Johnson stopped and looked at me.

I smiled back at him; for once, I was going to enjoy his visit.

"That happens sometimes when she gets upset," I consoled him. "Perhaps if you use her real name?" I said, without offering it to him.

"I'm sorry— er— Susie?" he said.

Kelly's Pandora's box of obscenities opened and filled the room.

Mr. Johnson moved on.

"Hello Pete," he said to Paul.

Paul, taking a cue from Kelly, got up and turned his desk over.

"Perhaps it's time for us to be going," Mr. Johnson said to the rest of the group, as he quickly headed for the door.

"Kelly, Paul, say hi to Mr. Johnson," I said, before he reached the door.

Immediately they stopped and said hello. Paul picked up his desk and Kelly returned to what she was doing.

I introduced the rest of my class to the group and explained that when Mr. Johnson called them by the wrong name it triggered the reaction they had witnessed.

All ended well, but I could tell by Mr. Johnson's stare that I had made an enemy. Somehow, it all seemed worth it.

Many times our trips to the community have left me pleasantly surprised with people's reactions.

I took my class to a hands-on museum one day. Everyone was enjoying the touch tunnel. This was actually a series of tunnels that people maneuvered through on all fours in the dark. I thought it would be a great experience. My students went in, one by one, and I followed the last student, Martin. Debbie waited at the other end with Ethan for us to exit.

Martin objected at first, but I urged him to try. I should not have done that. We made it ten yards into the tunnel when Martin stopped.

"Martin," I said, pushing his rear with my head. "Martin, are you all right?"

"There's a touch tunnel," Martin began. "There's the dark."

Martin's 250 pounds made my mild attempts to push him useless.

"Martin," I pleaded, as the students stacked up behind us. "Martin, you need to move."

"There's the carpet."

He wasn't budging. Luckily the tunnel was monitored for such events. The lights were turned on so Martin and I could exit the tunnel safely.

Martin immediately went to a bench and sat down. When two boys from another class sat next to him I was tempted to intercede before they made fun of him.

"Hi, my name is Bryan," one of the boys said. "What's yours?

I stayed back and watched.

"Martin," came his whispered reply.

"Martin, I just wanted to tell you that I was scared, too."

Then Bryan jumped up and ran to another part of the museum.

I'm not sure how much Martin took away from that situation. I left with a good feeling, having witnessed that there are kind, compassionate people in the world. I was glad to be part of it.

SOMETIMES, however, I have been completely fooled by people's reactions to our kids.

For a few years our county ran a program called Classroom in the Mall. We'd set up class for a day in local malls in the county. The objective was to give the community a first-hand look at what goes on in school. One year I took my class.

Since we would be there all day, we brought all our materials with us, including our record player to play music during some of our activities. We would eat lunch in one of the restaurants and everyone was excited about going.

Many people stopped and watched what was going on for a while; others would give us only a passing glance. One woman, in particular, caught my eye. For almost an hour she watched intently, straining to understand my students. Finally she approached me; I was ecstatic. Surely she saw what a great teacher I was and had a plethora of questions to ask. Perhaps I was even inspiring her to quit her current job and go into teaching. One thing was sure: I had certainly made an impression on her. This would be my moment to shine.

"Excuse me," she said politely.

"Yes," I said, pretending she took me by surprise.

"I have been watching your class for a while now and I wondered if I could ask you a question?"

"Sure," I said, readying myself with some pertinent information I was sure would complete the impression.

"Well, I was just wondering—"

"It's all right," I said, sensing her embarrassment at asking a question in front of my students.

I walked her a few yards away.

"I have been watching and listening and I was truly captivated," she continued.

My body ballooned with pride as I threw my chest out and smiled.

"Thank you," I responded.

"And I was just wondering if you could tell me what album you were playing? I just love it and I want to go right to the record store and buy it."

"Certainly," I said. Then her question sank in.

"Album?" I asked, as my balloon burst.

"Yes," she said, "could I see it?"

I walked over to the record player and brought her the album jacket.

"Here it is," I said, handing it to her.

She read it intently, wrote down the name of the performer, Dan Fogelberg, then returned it to me.

"Thank you," she said, handing it back to me.

I replaced the album and when I returned, she was gone.

I looked around to see if anyone else had noticed what had just happened. It looked safe.

"What did she want, Jim?" Debbie asked.

Perhaps she didn't hear. I was in the clear after all.

"Oh, nothing much," I said. "You know, just a question about the class."

"By the way, Jim," she continued, "do you think you can get me the name of the artist you'll be playing next? I'd love to go buy the album."

She laughed so hard I thought she was going to hurt herself.

I laughed, shook my head and vowed never to let it get that big again.

Extending the walls of our classroom helped us learn how to react to the new situations in which we found ourselves. We also learned that the rest of the people in the world react to us, and we needed to be aware of their reactions. Oh, sure, we stumbled occasionally, but we learned to pick ourselves up. The excitement of our new-found freedom urged us on.

Today, I find myself less worried about what other people are thinking about my students and me. We are no longer outsiders looking in. We have become part of the world, and the view from in here is wonderful!

Chapter Twenty-Two
Lank You, Tharue

*I*t is the indiscriminate nature of existence that we experience events that bring us joy and sorrow. Although we may prefer to wax nostalgic for the joyful memories, the painful ones have a place as well. They are often the vehicles that propel growth and development. At the very least, they enhance times of happiness or remind us of our mortality.

PAIN comes in many disguises; sometimes it is the words we use that cause pain.

Larue was a "normal" youngster until age three, when a car accident left her brain damaged. She was placed into special education and eventually found her way to my classroom. She was a beautiful young 14-year-old, stood 5'6" tall with long, light brown hair and big, beautiful green eyes. The accident stole some of her vision and a good deal of her ability to think and reason, but she retained a beautiful smile, a sense of humor and a gentleness that was unique to her.

Larue loved spoonerisms, the transposition of the initial sounds of words, such as Li Harue for Hi Larue. I was Yim Jerman, and the president was Cimmy Jarter and so forth. She loved to create her own and we'd play a game as we tried to one-up each other.

"Mood Gorning, Yister Merman," she'd say, as she entered the room.

"Lello Harue. Yow are hoo dotay?"

"Fine, yank thou."

We'd both laugh at our cleverness; I am not sure which one of us loved it more.

Larue was a very sensitive young lady, a fact drilled home to me one day when I least expected it. I have always been very careful not to raise my voice in frustration. When it really is necessary, I will do so, but I try to show my students that I am not angry with them, only with their behavior. I also push them to achieve and I certainly have no right to become angry when they are having difficulty. After all, it is my job to help them find ways to understand whatever it is we are teaching, not become irritated at them when they don't get it. However, I am human and sometimes, in spite of my good intentions, I make mistakes.

On this particular day, my body was in school but my mind was elsewhere. I was in the middle of a divorce, feeling sorry for myself and generally having a bad day.

Larue and I were working on math and she was just not understanding it. We had been over and over it, one way or another, and she was still not getting it. Normally I have the patience to help my students through such problems, but not on that day.

"Larue," I said adamantly. "You can do this. I know you can. Come on, THINK!"

Again she tried and again she failed.

"Larue!" I cried. "What is wrong with you today?"

I should have asked what was wrong with me.

Tears began to well up in her eyes.

"I'm sorry, Mr. Yerman," she said, wiping them away with her palm. "I'm OK. I'm OK. I can do it now. I know I can."

She attempted a halfhearted smile as the tears began to cascade down her cheeks.

I looked at Larue. Here sat a young, sweet, gentle girl who innocently looked to me for assistance. In a brief moment I had taken her trust, trampled on it and made her cry, all with a few callous words. She would never intentionally "not understand" a problem.

I felt about three inches tall. I took a deep breath and stepped toward her. She was still crying. Each tear dropped directly into my stomach, like acid.

"Larue," I said. "I am so sorry. I'm not angry with you. You are doing a wonderful job. Please forgive me."

I grabbed her paper.

"Let's forget about math for a while. What do you want to do?"

At that moment, she could have said anything and I would have agreed: a trip to Europe, a new car, a house, all she had to do was ask. Fortunately, she opted for a soda. We walked to the cafeteria and I bought her one. I spent the remainder of that day, and many more, trying to atone for my blunder.

Knowing I have the ability to help my students has always been a given to me. On that day, I was reminded I also have the ability to hurt them. The memory of her tears is forever etched in my mind. I only hope the same is not true for Larue.

Sometimes pain comes from the unlikeliest of places.

Osceola was situated on the West Coast of Florida. One of the best things about being there was that we were able to watch the space shuttle launches that started on the East Coast. We'd watch the countdown on television then hurry outside, hoping for a clear day so we could see the shuttle as it soared into the sky.

We were watching the day the Challenger exploded. I tend to avoid talking about death, especially with my students, but it was all over the news and the papers, so we discussed it in class. I didn't think my students had any problems until I received a call from Paul's mother.

"Jim, I called to tell you that Paul's depressed and I don't know what to do."

"How do you know he's depressed?" I asked. Anyone who knew Paul knew that he generally looked and acted depressed.

"He just seems to be down," was her reply.

"What do you think he's depressed about?" I asked.

"After the Challenger, he thinks he's going to die and he wants to know when. I don't know what to do," she said.

"Let me talk to him tomorrow," I said.

When Paul came to school the next day I asked him about it.

"Your mother said you were upset about the Challenger," I began.

Paul didn't answer.

"She said you're sad."

Again no answer, but he began that familiar movement of his head.

"She said you are wondering when you are going to die."

"Yes," he said, looking up at me. "Yes, Mr. Yerman."

Two options seemed clear to me. I could tell him the truth: that no one knows when he or she is going to die. Or, I could lie. Knowing Paul's inclination to worry and his rigidity, my choice was clear.

"Paul," I said, "I know when you're going to die."

He sat up.

I took out the calendar for effect.

"Let's see. Hmm. Yes, here it is. You will die on February 21 in the year 2159."

I didn't tell him he would be 180 years old at the time. Why compound a lie with the truth?

A wave of relief swept over him and he smiled.

"Jim, what did you say to him?" his mom asked on the phone that night. "He's completely changed."

I told her about my little white lie and we laughed at its simplicity.

"You know," she said, "he probably will live to be 180."

"I wouldn't put it past him," I said. "He's just stubborn enough to do it."

DEALING with Larue and Paul's pain was relatively simple. When death hit a little closer to home, it was more difficult.

Ethan's Muscular Dystrophy finally took him during his 17th year of life. I was in North Carolina with my wife Deborah, on spring vacation, when I received the news. We hiked to the top of a mountain, planted a little cross, covered it with flowers and cried. I was going to miss him.

When I returned from vacation I visited his mother. She explained how Ethan had caught a cold that quickly developed into pneumonia (something common in MD patients). She took him to the doctor and was cleared to take him home and monitor him. Ethan was sitting in his favorite chair that same evening, when he started having trouble breathing. Gently, she moved her arms around him and cradled him to her chest, as she had done a hundred times before. It was there, nestled in his mother's bosom, where he was always safe and happy, that he died.

Back in class we talked about Ethan's death, that it meant we would no longer see him and that we were going to miss him. My students noticed how sad I was. I told them that feeling sad about death was perfectly normal. Closing our discussion, we each took turns remembering something special about Ethan. It was the best way that I could think of to say goodbye.

Ethan's mother bequeathed many of Ethan's belongings to my classroom. She gave us his record collection and tapes and a framed picture of Ethan that I still have. She also gave me the one item I hold dearest in my entire teaching career. Listed in Ethan's obituary, after his address and cause of death, she had written that he was a student at Osceola Middle School in Mr. Jim Yerman's Autistic class. To this day, I carry it with me wherever I go, laminated and tucked safely in my wallet.

After saying goodbye to Ethan, we soon had two more goodbyes to go through. Lenny and Jack had turned 21 and they were graduating.

Since ours was the only autistic program in a regular school in our county, there was no formal graduation ceremony. We had maintained ties to Nina and graduated our students with theirs.

Lenny and Jack were lucky. A new employment training program had recently started in our county for people with disabilities. Lenny and Jack were accepted into the program and received job training. Lenny ended up working at Pizza Hut and Jack at Red Lobster. While I was sad to see them go, I was very proud of them both.

One of life's greatest pleasures is the gift of reminiscing. Anytime, anywhere, we can call up a fond memory and relive a time that brought us great joy or even one that caused us sorrow. Whether it happens in response to some trigger, or we purposely bring it forth, memories connect us with the people and places and events that were truly meaningful in our life.

I cannot drive by a Red Lobster or a Pizza Hut without thinking about Jack and Lenny.

Each time I watch a space shuttle take off, I wonder how Paul is doing.

I cannot open my wallet without thinking of Ethan.

Not a day goes by that I don't think about the students who have crossed my path. They are the ancestors of the students I teach today, the pioneers who courageously joined me in our journey through uncharted territory. I remember each of their lessons and thank them for everything they have given me.

Thank you, Lenny and Jack.

Thank you, Paul.

Thank you, Ethan.

Oh, and Lank you, Tharue, wherever you are.

Chapter Twenty-Three

Letting Go

One day when I was a child, I found a baby bird fluttering on the ground. She was too young to fly so I rushed her home and made her a nest inside a cardboard box. Using an eyedropper I was able to nurse her back to health. When she seemed ready, I stood near the woods by my back door, gently cradled her with both hands and tenderly tossed her into the air. Her wings flapped a couple of times, then off she flew into the sky.

Parenting, and to a certain degree teaching, are like taking care of that little bird. While we might prefer to protect our children forever, it is our job to nurture them and teach them until they are ready to fly. There comes a day when we need to stand aside and let them take off.

With handicapped children, nothing is more important or more difficult to do than to know when to let go. Many of the students I teach are endowed with a permanent innocence that, in many cases, will prevent them from becoming totally independent. Both parents and teachers often walk a fine line between expecting too much or too little, helping too much or not enough, between creating frustration or dependence. If these children are ever to achieve independence successfully— no matter to what degree—it is a challenge we must take up, a line we must walk.

There is no easy formula for knowing when to push harder and when to stand back. It is a totally subjective decision, formulated by our brain, with our heart as an advisor. They don't always agree on what to do.

There have been times when I have chosen not to intervene and I've watched my student's independence shine like a full moon on a cloudless night.

For instance, many of my male students pull their pants down to use the restroom. I have taught them to use a stall and close the door. On one trip to the the mall I was accompanying a group of my students to the restroom. They had scurried ahead of me and I walked in at the same time as another gentleman, whom I did not know. All the stalls were occupied so my students were standing at the urinals, all five of them, with their pants down, as the older gentleman and I walked in.

"Can you believe this?" the man grunted to me, as we entered the restroom.

Since nature was already taking its course and it was too late to rectify the situation, I quickly decided this was one of those times I would let my students stand on their own.

"No, I can't," I answered, looking around. "I wonder who their teacher is?"

Fortunately my new acquaintance was in a stall when my students finished and I ushered them back into the mall.

Another time we were at our local grocery store and my students were all working on various tasks. Non-talking Lenny was standing with me near an unoccupied check out line. He stood next to the cash register, smiling. I would show him a picture of an item I wanted him to find in the store. He'd then go and look for it. On this particular day he was wearing his usual attire, a white T-shirt and blue jeans. Despite the fact that we were far removed from the open check out lines, the closed sign was posted, the lights were turned out, and we certainly didn't look like store employees, people would pull their carts up to the register and want us to check them out. Usually we would politely tell them the aisle was closed and that would be the end of that.

On this particular day, I was busy with another student while Lenny was waiting for me at his spot near the cash register.

Before I realized it a man pushed his cart up to the register.

"Hey, are you going to check me out?" he asked Lenny.

I heard his question, turned to intercede, and then for some reason, stopped myself. I wanted to see how long it would take this man to comprehend the situation.

Lenny also heard the question and answered with a nod of his head, his usual way of responding to questions.

The man began putting his groceries on the conveyor that was not moving.

"Well, are you going to check me out or what?" he asked again, after Lenny made no attempt to ring him up.

Lenny shook his head again and smiled.

"I'm sorry, sir," I said finally. "This aisle isn't open."

"Not open?" he grumbled. "What do you mean, not open? This young man told me he was open."

"I'm sorry, sir, but this young man doesn't talk," I said.

He looked at Lenny. Lenny smiled and shook his head.

"Isn't open, can't talk, what kind of store is this?" I heard him mumble, as he restocked his cart and walked away.

Lenny looked at me and smiled.

I probably should have stepped in sooner, but I was sure the man would catch on to what was happening. The fact that he didn't gave me some solace. If a man could mistake a 6'2" non-verbal young man wearing a T-shirt and blue jeans for a cashier, and carry on a conversation with him, then perhaps we were becoming a part of the community after all.

MOST of my teaching life has been spent giving my students opportunities to make their own decisions and find their own way. It has led to many funny and surreal moments and luckily, no one has been harmed. In fact, they have helped me deal with the inherent sadness of autism, a disability that robs so much from so many people.

There have been times, however, when my experiences with autistic students have been neither funny nor surreal.

One day, out of the blue, Larue began crying. I asked her what was wrong, but she was unable to express herself with any degree of clarity. She just kept crying. Finally, remembering she loved to draw, I asked her to write or draw what was bothering her.

When she was finished I walked over to her desk.

"May I see what you've done?" I asked.

Her eyes, wide open, were reddened with tears. She wiped the vestiges of grief from her cheeks and handed me the paper.

I raised the paper and began reading, only to stop abruptly.

I took a deep breath then looked up to the heavens for support. I was looking at what I thought was proof that Larue was being sexually abused.

She had written some clear and concise sentences.

"No, please, don't."

"I don't want to anymore."

"Don't put your pecker in my cooter."

"I don't want to anymore."

I closed my eyes for a second. Although I was filling with rage, I had an innocent young lady in front of me who needed my compassion, not my anger. I knew she would misunderstand the anger.

"Larue, do you feel like writing anymore?" I asked. I wanted to be sure that she was coming up with this information on her own.

"OK," she said.

She took the paper and began writing again.

This gave me a few minutes to think. I knew I had to report what Larue was saying, but I wasn't sure what to say to her. I was sure she was unhappy and uncomfortable with what had happened to her, but at the same time, I wasn't sure how much she really understood.

Larue lived alone with her father and I was sure he wouldn't do anything to harm her. I was relatively sure it was one of her father's friends who hung around the house.

"I'm finished, Mr. Yerman," Larue said, breaking my train of thought.

Again she handed me the paper.

"Please get off me."

"No, no, no more."

"I don't want to kiss anymore."

"Don't tell anyone about this."

On and on the sentences filled the page as my fury swelled deeper and deeper. Taking advantage of an innocent, defenseless child is unforgivable.

"Larue," I said, looking into her eyes and searching for the correct words. "I'm sorry you're so sad. You were right to say "no." You will always be right to say "no." What this person did was wrong and I will try to help you. If it happens again, you say "no" and let me know, OK?"

Larue looked at me and smiled.

"OK, Yister Merman. I will."

With that, she forgot about her problem for the moment and began concentrating on her schoolwork.

I immediately reported this to the assistant principal. He gave the papers to the police and they began an investigation.

One of the most difficult things I have ever done was watch Larue go home on the bus that day. I had told her I would help her, yet I was letting her go back to the same house where she was molested. As I walked her to the bus I reminded her that she can and should say "no." Watching her ride away, smiling and waving, made my heart drop. My only hope was that the police were on top of the situation.

After a restless night, I arrived at school the next day, greeted by a detective from the local police department.

He had tried to interview Larue, to no avail.

"I'm afraid Larue didn't give us anything consistent. I'm sure something happened but she couldn't tell me much about what happened or who might have done it. She is very sweet but difficult to understand."

"I understand detective. What do we do from here?"

"Nothing, I'm afraid," he said.

"Nothing!"

"There's really nothing we can do. We certainly don't have enough evidence to arrest anyone. We have to wait. I have spoken with Larue's father and he assures me nothing happened. He may be lying or he may not know. At any rate, he is aware that we will be watching. It's the best we can do."

"And what about Larue?" I asked.

"She goes home today, same as always."

The day before, as I had watched her ride home on the bus, I was angry. Today I was frustrated and felt helpless and inadequate.

That night I contacted Larue's older sister, Lonnie, who lived nearby. She said she would go over immediately and get Larue and that she could live with her until she could contact her mother, who lived about five hours away in North Florida.

I was pleased. Larue was going to have some relief after all.

She lived with Lonnie for the rest of the school year and was happy as a lark. She never again spoke of that night and I was happy no permanent damage was done.

In many ways my students are like the injured baby bird I found when I was a boy. We need to know when to help them and when to let them go. So many times the everyday decisions we make in life are unimportant and affect us only mildly. But there are times when the decisions we make directly affect another person's life. As teachers, we have an awesome responsibility and mustn't treat it lightly.

Larue moved in with her mother over the summer and I never saw her again. Lonnie occasionally called to let me know she was living on a farm and very happy.

I was unhappy that Larue left and very sad that I didn't have a chance to say goodbye. But that's the way it is sometimes, when they decide to flap their wings.

Chapter Twenty-Four

So You Want to be a Teacher?

As fate would have it, our next school year began again in another new school. The county autism program had grown so quickly that a high school unit was needed. Since many of my students were of high school age, we were elected to move to Osceola High, just across the street from Osceola Middle.

It was sad to start without Larue, but my mind was quickly occupied with a batch of new students and my first official intern.

She arrived about two weeks into the year.

"So, you want to teach kids with autism?" I asked her.

"Yes, I think so," she said.

"Well, there's a good place to start," I said, pointing at Richie, a new student who had run by us and out the door. He was quickly heading down the hall.

"His name is Ritchie; he's a runner. You need to get him and bring him back."

She hesitated.

"And you better hurry," I said, looking toward the door.

I could only guess what was running through her mind at that moment. Perhaps she was wondering what in the world she was doing there, what circumstances had brought her to that exact spot at that exact time.

Me? I was thinking about how life travels in circles. As I watched her run after Richie, I was thinking about all the great teachers I've had over the years.

As I stood in the doorway, I couldn't help but smile at the sight of my intern bringing Richie back to the fold.

"Nice catch," I said. "By the way, my name is Mr. Yerman."

"Mine's Nancy."

"Nice to meet you, Nancy."

With our exchange of pleasantries, Richie took off again.

Nancy looked at me, rolled her eyes, and took off after him.

I didn't have the chance to impart any great words of wisdom as she sped away, but I tried anyway.

"So you want to be a teacher?" I whispered, as she rounded the corner out of sight.

"You'd better hold on tight. You're in for a wild ride!"

A little work, a little play
To keep us going—and so good day!

A little warmth, a little light
Of love's bestowing—and so good night!

A little fun, to match the sorrow
Of each day's growing—and so good morrow!

A little trust that when we die
We reap our sowing! And so goodbye!

George Du Maurier

Printed in the United States
80814LV00004B/1-114

9 781885 477743